What Our Lettering Needs

T0338910

Rick Cusick

The Contribution of Hermann Zapf

What Our Lettering Needs

to Calligraphy & Type Design

at Hallmark Cards

Preface by Sumner Stone

RIT CARY GRAPHIC ARTS PRESS · MMXI

Published and distributed by:
Cary Graphic Arts Press
90 Lomb Memorial Drive
Rochester, New York 14623
http://carypress.rit.edu

Printed in the U. S.

ISBN 978-1-933360-55-3

Cover: The paste papers reproduced on the cover were provided by Hermann Zapf
in 1973 for the Hallmark book, *Favorite Bible Verses*, but were not used. The quotation,
set in Hallmark Stratford, is from *About Alphabets* (1960). Photograph by Jill Bell.
Cover Design: Rick Cusick

Library of Congress Cataloging-in-Publication Data

What our lettering needs: the contribution of Hermann Zapf to calligraphy & type design
at Hallmark Cards / Rick Cusick
      p. cm.
      Includes bibliographical references and index.
      ISBN 978-1-933360-55-3 (alk. paper)
1. Zapf, Hermann. 2. Type and type-founding—History—20th century. 3. Calligraphy—
History—20th century. 4. Hallmark Cards, Inc. I. Title. II. Title: Contribution of Hermann
Zapf to calligraphy and type design at Hallmark Cards.
      Z250.A2Z374 2011
      686.2'210904—dc23
                             2011016335

We can best express

our respect for the great achievements of the past

by aiming toward expressing the spirit of the present,

honest and just to our day. | HZ

Contents

Notes on Chapter Openings

Frontispiece ii
Informal alphabet by HZ, proposed by Myron McVay and David Welty
for a wall design at Hallmark, reinterpreted for this publication.

What Our Lettering Needs xvi
Photograph of Hallmark headquarters building in Kansas City (circle in-
dicating location of the penthouse) and two views of HZ's studio on the
Main River. Guestbook entry by HZ during his first visit to Hallmark.

The Art of Hermann Zapf & *Its Effects 12*
Photographs taken during the filming of *The Art of Hermann Zapf*; still
showing writing on acetate; and diagram from the movie. Also, photographs of two props used in the film.

The Lettering Manual 24
Page with diagram by HZ suggesting proper mixing of typefaces. Sketch
for the title page and various details from the manual.

Typographic Transition 32
Photograph of HZ. Final drawings for Firenzi, Hallmark Textura, and
Hallmark Uncial; proof of Missouri with corrections. An interpretation
of the 18-unit grid used to determine spacing for photocomposition.

Hallmark Editions 66
Title spreads from the early days of the book line. Drawing by Bill Greer
used on the end liners for *The Sweet Love Remembered.* Alternate title lettering by HZ for *Favorite Bible Verses* and the Chi Rho used on the back
dust jacket. Indication of "Hallmark Editions" by HZ from a mock-up.

Unfinished Projects 81
Proposals for acetate posters by HZ damaged in the mail. A letter to J.C.
Hall with HZ's thoughts on a proposed museum of lettering. Very
rough sketch for a title page by HZ for a projected Hallmark Bible.

More Than a Business Relationship 88
Candid photos of HZ with Noel Gordon and Harald Peter. Photo of HZ,
Myron McVay, and Marshall Wagoner during a lecture at Hallmark.
Detail of the door to HZ's studio in Darmstadt made of woodtype and
a ball-point warm-up exercise by HZ given to Noel Gordon.

Preface: Zapf at Hallmark

The lights went down and the film began. There, standing in front of a blackboard, a thin, upright man in a dark suit made a sweeping gesture with his right hand, and behind the hand there appeared a vapor trail of blue chalk and then another and another. It was the letter A. I was, in the argot of my student life, blown away—by the controlled but graceful movements and, simultaneously, by the beauty of the form. Then came the equally elegant B. With each stroke, my attention became more firmly riveted. Within a few minutes, a magical dancing alphabet creature had been conjured on the blackboard by this genius of letters. I was in a trance. Then, using different tools, more gorgeous letters appeared from his firm but delicate hand. Finally, when the lights came up, I came back to earth. I was sitting in my first calligraphy class watching a film showing Hermann Zapf at work. The film had been made by Hallmark Cards.

Although Hallmark no longer makes the film available for loan, it is included on the CD for Linotype Zapfino.

That was almost forty years ago. The vivid impression has lasted. I can still run the movie in my mind's eye. Not only did watching Professor Zapf's performance broaden my perspective on making letters, it set off a chain of events that started me on my career as a professional letter maker.

I soon learned that Hallmark hired people to do lettering. I could not believe that there was a place that actually paid people to make letters. Not only that, it was rumored that Hermann Zapf himself visited Hallmark on a regular basis as a consultant who, among other things, worked with the lettering artists.

Making a portfolio took me about six months. I had a little experience even before my first formal letterform education in Lloyd Reynolds's class at Reed College, but I was still a relative novice. I did not know what to expect, but Hallmark called and asked me to fly out to Kansas City for an interview. By the end of the summer, I was driving east in a VW bus packed like a sardine can with all of my possessions, bound for Kansas City, home of Hallmark.

Reynolds was at Reed College for 50 years revealing the interconnectedness of things, reminding his students that "all distances are within reach."

Not only did Zapf show up, he turned out to be approachable and sympathetic. He spent time with each person in the lettering department. He gave lectures and demonstrations for us. He commiserated with our plight as thc lowliest members of the creative staff. He tried to show us more efficient ways of working and to instill in us the sense of beauty and discipline that characterized his own work. He started work on a training manual for the lettering artists and made short instructional films showing his special ways of handling the metal broad-edged pen and the ballpoint.

It was during this period that I was introduced to the process of making type. Hermann was designing faces for Hallmark's proprietary use. I did not participate directly in the process, but I did get to look over some shoulders. I was both fascinated and surprised by the production process. The Zapf drawings had to be positioned, spaced, tested, and adjusted until they took their places on a small film font "grid" used to set type with the lettering department's newly acquired phototypesetting machine.

There was a calligraphic italic called Firenze, the subtle Crown Roman in which this book is set, and an unusual, edged-pen concoction dubbed Missouri, among others. They all had the Zapfian pixie dust on them, and I was enchanted to be in the place where they were being made, tested, and, for the first time, typeset.

The enchantment was tempered every time it was my turn for "retouch"—a day devoted to removing the specks on the typographic prints produced by dust in the phototypesetter. The task was performed with a small, pointed watercolor brush and either opaque white or black, depending on whether the offending intruder was inside or outside the letter. It was a good exercise in precision with the tool. I later learned that Hermann himself started out as a photo retoucher.

There were the broadsides he made one day, quickly written on small pieces of paper and then, all in the same day, drastically enlarged and screen printed downstairs in the printing lab (in the same big building that housed all the art, editorial, and prepress production areas). I thought these were treasures. I still have one.

I recall one episode in which he was asked to design the stationery for the president of the company. It consisted very simply of the name Don Hall, set in Optima, centered at the top of the page. Hermann pasted up each letter. He then put the pasteup on the floor and stared at it for a long time. Then he made a tiny adjustment followed by another long stare at the piece on the floor. This time he was standing on a chair. Then another tiny adjustment. Then more staring...

This was one of many observations that helped me understand the underlying process that was needed to create the objects I found so appealing. Sometimes the process happened quickly and sometimes slowly, but behind it there was always the high energy and the intense focus. I was at Hallmark for less than two years, during which Hermann appeared only a few times for a few weeks. Not much time really, but it had a profound effect on my view of how letters were made, and it gave momentum to my nascent efforts to pursue The Letter.

Rick Cusick has been, besides Hermann himself, the motivating force behind this book and has spent years collecting and corresponding, reconstructing the Zapf at Hallmark phenomenon. It is a real pleasure to see the result of this effort—the little-known work Hermann did at Hallmark finally receiving some of the attention it richly deserves. Zapf's efforts there were not confined to the type designs, graphic designs, book designs, and teaching materials he produced, although these are certainly important. He also inspired and taught. Rick and I were among the young lettering artists who had the great good fortune to participate in the experience. Happily, this book now makes the Hallmark material, so influential in my own life, available to a much wider audience.

Sumner Stone / Guinda, California

Photograph taken while filming the opening sequence
of *The Art of Hermann Zapf*

Introduction

Although the idea for a book about Hermann Zapf's relationship with Hallmark was formed more than a decade ago in San Francisco, the events that led up to this book began more than four decades ago and eighty miles away, in Stockton, California, my hometown. In 1969, I had just begun my professional life with letters, designing illuminated signs for AdArt, Inc., whose headquarters and main manufacturing plant was in Stockton. At the time, AdArt was one of the firms most responsible for transforming the casinos of Las Vegas and other parts of the Nevada landscape into spectacular displays of imagination and light.

First-rate talent complemented the general good humor of the small AdArt staff, directed by Chuck Barnard, who hired me believing that my interest in lettering would make up for my lack of experience in design. All of them made it look easy.

I was thankful for the job and the opportunity to work with a staff of designers who routinely created magic with such diverse materials as plastic, neon, and extruded aluminum. Walking through the shop and yard among the fabricated letters and signs, some much taller than me, only added to my fascination. But I had thoughts on a smaller scale. As an aspiring book designer and lettering artist, I was interested in learning more about designing for the printed page. So, among other things, I began corresponding with a number of designers and calligraphers, asking mainly for the titles of books they would recommend.

Hermann responded to my query with a cordial letter, including a letterpress version of his well-known Cobden-Sanderson quotation regarding "the whole duty of typography"[1] and a list of his publications, at the bottom of which was mentioned the movie, *The Art of Hermann Zapf*, produced by Hallmark and available for loan from the company. I borrowed the film numerous times (to study Hermann's technique) while working at AdArt and later while attending Art Center College of Design in Los Angeles—so often, in fact, that someone at Hallmark became curious enough to call and invite me to Kansas City for an interview. A job offer soon followed. So it was that my friendship with Hermann Zapf began more than two years before we would actually meet at Hallmark's headquarters.

In the fall of 2001, an exhibition and series of events and lectures honoring Hermann and Gudrun Zapf's contributions to type design was held at the San Francisco Public Library. During a break in the opening festivities of this "Zapfest," I spoke with them about the possibility of producing a small book regarding the alphabets they designed for Hallmark in the late '60s and early '70s. They liked the idea and graciously offered their support. However, not long into the project, it became clear to me that a more comprehensive account of this period in Hermann's life, including something about the people, conditions, and events that surrounded it, might be worthwhile—offering an opportunity to contribute new information to an already remarkably well-documented career. Also, because it is inextricably linked to this time, I felt a few words about Hermann's friendship and work with the late Phil Metzger, proprietor of the Crabgrass Press, would be appropriate. These can be found in the appendix.

During the past thirty years, it has been my pleasure to provide upon request most of what has been written about the Hallmark/Zapf association, beginning in the late '70s when Paul Vandervoort asked me for material for the Zapf installment of his "Calligraphy" series in *Signs of the Times* magazine.[2] In 1989, I contributed the essay "Kansas City and Hallmark" to the festschrift *ABC-XYZapf*, edited by John Dreyfus and Knut Erichson.[3] And more recently, I spoke about "The Kansas City Connection" for the Society of Typographic Aficionados as part of their tribute to Hermann Zapf at TypeCon/2003 in Minneapolis.

The following account draws on all of these efforts but mostly on my contribution to *Calligraphic Type Design in the Digital Age*, the catalog edited by John Prestianni that accompanied the exhibition at Zapfest.[4] That article, "Cultivating an Education in Letters," was necessarily restricted by time and the conventions of an anthology, not to mention the limitations of the author. Two of the three have been rectified with this publication. I have had ample time to delve deeper into the Hallmark archives than ever before and to contact former employees who had firsthand experience of some of the events related here. In some cases they had their own archives to draw on—invaluable for extracting facts from hearsay and hazy recollections. Still, there is no denying the inevitable fog that accompanies the passage of time.

("After all," as Hermann reminded me, "it's been more than forty years."[5]) No less frustrating is the realization that as a company like Hallmark becomes a company like Hallmark, and the day-to-day activities of doing business turn into years, then decades, and now a full century, potential archival material is often unrecognized and sometimes lost. Such has been the case with items pertinent to this study.

Because I knew or worked with many of the individuals mentioned in this book (both inside and outside of Hallmark), preparing it has been somewhat like hosting a reunion of remarkable talents with Hermann as the guest of honor. While acknowledging their many contributions, I have done my best to avoid nostalgic exaggerations associated with most reunions. The events covered reflect a particularly vital period in the company's evolution, when the ideas and dreams of Hallmark founder J. C. Hall and his son and successor, Donald Hall Sr., were matched by the means to accommodate them. Hermann's stint as a consultant to the company was a valuable part of this prosperous time—its influence lasting long after the formal connection ended and ranging well beyond the company's confines.

Donald Hall, Sr. is now co-chairman of the board. Today the company is led by J. C. Hall's grandsons, Donald Hall, Jr., president and CEO, and David Hall, president, Hallmark North America

And while this book is an appreciation of Hermann's contributions to Hallmark, now fully blended into the company's heritage, it is also a reminder of his belief which I first heard in *The Art of Hermann Zapf,* that the artist's challenge is "to ensure, despite technology and mass production, that beauty is never lost."

Rick Cusick / Kansas City, Missouri
November 2011

November 20th
1965

Hermann Zapf
Frankfurt am Main

ONE: WHAT OUR LETTERING NEEDS

Of the many firsts that Hermann Zapf experienced during his annual visits to Hallmark Cards' headquarters in Kansas City, one of the most memorable was tracking the funnel cloud of a tornado from the company's tenth-floor penthouse. Others were less mesmeric. He remembers the first major league baseball game he attended as slow and confusing and that "everyone was sad at the end because we lost," a common outcome for the Kansas City A's, arguably one of the worst teams in major league baseball history. During another visit, a Hallmark executive persuaded Zapf to try horseback riding with him and his two young daughters, assuring Hermann that the mount he would be riding was docile and well-trained. Zapf recalls it was neither: "The horse did not follow my instructions and headed straight for thorny bushes. I had no idea how to jump from it without breaking my neck!"[1]

But if the sight of Hermann Zapf astride a runaway horse seems improbable, so, it might have appeared, was the relationship between one of the world's most celebrated masters of type design, calligraphy, and book design—especially admired for his own fine limited editions—and the world's leading manufacturer of greeting cards, whose print run of a single design can number into the tens of thousands. Nevertheless, the relationship began in 1965 when Zapf was invited to visit Hallmark's headquarters by Hans Archenhold, then head of the firm's graphic arts division. According to Archenhold, Hallmark president and founder J. C. Hall "immediately took to Hermann and appreciated his work."[2] Jeannette Lee, retired vice-president of corporate design, told me many years later that it was Zapf's "quality and refined good taste"[3] that Hall admired, attributes that would allow Zapf over the next few years to quietly influence Hallmark in unmistakable ways.

A 1976 article in Publishers Weekly about Hallmark books reported that a first printing ranged from 25,000 to 50,000 copies.

Common Ground

J. C. Hall had an instinct for quality. His quest for "the very best" prompted him to consult with the brightest minds on a variety of corporate matters—from marketing strategies to retail design to the planning of a large urban commercial and residential complex. Among the international creative community, he conferred with such like-minded visionaries as Henry Dreyfuss, Raymond Loewy, Charles and Ray Eames, Walt Disney, and Edward Durrell Stone, to name a few. The quote "I'm hell-bent on quality,"[4] attributed to Hall, can be reasoned as no mere boast.

Hall also commissioned art for his products from a variety of well-known artists and illustrators, some more obvious choices than others, including Norman Rockwell, Grandma Moses, Salvador Dali and Saul Steinberg.

His persistence naturally included searching for ways to improve the quality of Hallmark products, and he had specific ideas about the use of lettering and typography for those products, especially greeting cards. A business whose editorial content largely focuses on human relationships and the most significant events in the course of a lifetime must be concerned with how that content is presented.

In 1964, Hall wrote a memorandum entitled "What Our Lettering Needs" that expressed his thoughts on the subject in a way that allowed for individual interpretation. Points from the memo included:

- Lettering should be simple and clear and in the most attractive style.
- The style of the caption should suit both the design and the caption subject.
- Lettering should detract from the appearance of the cover as little as possible.[5]

The caption on the cover of a greeting card identifies the occasion and often the recipient, i.e., "Happy Anniversary, Mom and Dad."

A few cynics on staff joked that this last point was a parapraxis, revealing Hall's true feelings, i.e., "Too bad lettering has to be on the cover at all!"

Apparently aware that lettering is no more immune to fashion and affectation than any other form of design, Hall further stated that "we should attempt to get a 'new' look without being extreme."[6] This wasn't so much a reflection of his conservative nature as it was his understanding of the importance of clearly communicating to the reader. It speaks indirectly to a familiar axiom at Hallmark: a card is picked up by a consumer for what it looks like but is purchased for what it says. The primary role of a lettering artist or designer is to enhance the experience.

Although Hall's emphasis on clarity and suitability, essentially commonsense typography, is reminiscent of scholar and writer Beatrice Warde's dictum, "Printing should be invisible,"[7] it doesn't entirely reject the expressive possibilities of letterforms. One of the more interesting aspects in designing with lettering and type on greeting cards and other products such as books, calendars, and albums is the range required to handle a variety of editorial voices—from quiet restraint to more lively solutions, including humorous ones. Certainly, nothing in Hall's memo would have conflicted with Zapf's philosophy.

According to Noel Gordon, an accomplished Hallmark lettering artist and art director whose growing responsibilities at the time included directing lettering and typography, Hall's memo opened up discussions that eventually led to the notion of finding "a worthy consultant for our Lettering Department."[8] After some discussion, the decision was made to approach Zapf.

Jim Berry and Rick Ywwearick followed Noel as managers of Lettering during Hermann's tenure as a consultant.

Earlier Lettering Influences

This wasn't the first time that J. C. Hall had expressed an interest in outstanding artists skilled in lettering. In the late 1940s, he retained Austrian émigré Andrew Szoeke to design products and provide inspiration to the Hallmark design staff after seeing some of Szoeke's lettering in the windows of Bergdorf Goodman in New York. Trained in industrial design, Szoeke was a self-taught calligrapher and versatile designer with a penchant for oversized

business cards featuring deeply embossed and finely engraved lettering. (This style influenced Hallmark products for many years.) Szoeke moved to New York in 1921 and, though quiet and reclusive, built up a prestigious clientele that included major ad

Overleaf: One of
Szeoke's business cards

Andrew Szoeke in his
Manhattan studio

agencies, magazines such as *Vanity Fair* and *Harper's Bazaar,* and
retailers like Bergdorf Goodman, Macy's, and Saks Fifth Avenue.

Also, Szoeke operated a second business on Long Island with
his son, making custom furniture and accessories that featured
marquetry of his lettering and designs. Coincidently, two young
New York artists destined for future success in the lettering arts
had connections with that endeavor. Calligrapher Alice Koeth,
well known for her work for Steuben Glass and the Pierpont
Morgan Library, told me that her first job after college was cutting letters out of wood for Szoeke. And Ed Benguiat, legendary
type designer and lettering artist, recently told me that when he
was just starting out, Szoeke hired him to design the package in
which some of the wooden accessories were sold. (Szoeke provided
the graphics.)

Szoeke was an avid collector of printed matter, both ephem-
eral and rare, much of which was acquired by Hallmark after his
death in 1969. This work, as well as a considerable amount of his

4

Lettering by Andrew Szoeke, including
an example of his marquetry, and an
early version of the Hallmark Cards logo

own lettering and design, resides in the Hallmark archives as a resource for the staff and a reminder of his many contributions to the company, though they need look no farther than the back of a Hallmark card. It was Szoeke who in 1948 provided the

original inspiration for the familiar "crown Hallmark" logo, now one of the most recognized marks in the world. (It was registered by the company in 1949.)

During this period, Hall was also interested in Mortimer Leach, another influential lettering artist who, after having enjoyed success in New York, had moved to southern California in the late 1940s. When I was studying with him at Art Center in 1971, Leach told me that some years earlier he had turned down an offer from Hall to manage Hallmark's Lettering Department. The author of the classic *Lettering for Advertising* (a familiar book at Hallmark), he was well respected as a lettering artist and educator and would have been a valuable asset to the corporation.

Photograph of original lettering by Mortimer Leach used in his book *Lettering for Advertising*

Right: Leach and Rick Cusick in Leach's studio in early 1971, with HZ's broadside "The Art Director's Story" faintly visible on the wall behind them

6

Original English version of "The Art Director's Story" designed by HZ in 1960

While not really an advocate of calligraphy (he saw little use for it in the advertising world for which he did most of his work), he appreciated it enough to include examples by, among others, Lou Frimkess, Maury Nemoy, and Byron J. Macdonald in his second book, *Lettering in the Graphic Arts.*

In class and also during our chats over coffee, Leach spoke highly of Zapf's work, expressing particular admiration for his type designs. When I visited him in his studio at home, he was quick to point out a type specimen hanging on the wall set in Zapf's Palatino. It was an adaptation of Hermann's, "The Art Director's Story," a humorous account of what can happen to an otherwise great idea once a committee gets hold of it. It is reasonable to assume that had Leach accepted Hall's offer, he would have been enthusiastic about a Hallmark/Zapf association, es-

Hermann designed the original broadside, with drawings by Erwin Poell, for the Stempel typefoundry in 1960.

pecially considering the number of alphabets Hermann eventually designed for the company.

Hallmark Emissary

As stated earlier, the man who initiated the contact with Zapf was Hans Archenhold. Archenhold, who died in 1998 at age 93, was known as a tough taskmaster with a passion for quality. His association with Hallmark began on a snowy morning in 1940 when he arrived unannounced at headquarters hoping to see Mr. Hall. Hall gives the following account of their initial meeting in his informal memoir, *When You Care Enough*:

> The receptionist called to say there was a man who wanted to see me to discuss lithography. The gentleman had an extraordinary tale.... He was the son-in-law of the principal owner of the biggest and best greeting card plant in Europe. Hitler had sent him and members of his family to...Dachau, and the Nazis had taken over the plant to build Messerschmitt fighter planes. Colonel Josiah Wedgwood of the famous Wedgwood china family had helped Archenhold escape from Germany. Hans was in London when he saw the Hallmark display at Selfridge's, the department store. Then and there he decided he wanted to work for us and came directly to Kansas City from London.... He was recognized in the lithographic industry as one of the top men in Germany, a country famous for fine lithography. He had the highest standards of quality and had worked continuously to improve the lithographic process. I liked Hans and asked him to join our organization.[9]

With his printing background, Archenhold brought considerable knowledge of art history, color, and engineering with him. And eventually, J. C. Hall put it to good use. When the United States entered World War II, Hall, certain that the quality of goods manufactured in the nation would be worsened because of material shortages and other restrictions, gave Archenhold the responsibility of improving the quality of Hallmark cards. Hall was notably pleased with the results and, thereafter, Hans was known at Hallmark as having made printing an art.

In fact, Archenhold spent most of his fifty-year association with the company searching for ways to improve not only the quality of printing on Hallmark products but, as he would say, the "quality of life" for key employees by guiding them on tours through the great museums, galleries, and concert halls of the world—a program the organization has continued in his memory. But Archenhold believed and stated in a 1992 interview that one of the most important things he did for the organization was to "bring in Hermann Zapf." He summed up the matter with: "Hermann Zapf is a genius in typography like Mozart was in music."[10]

Zapf's Initial Visit

According to Zapf, Archenhold first met with him in Frankfurt, and after having "raved about the quality at Hallmark and how nice everyone there was,"[11] suggested Hermann visit Kansas City to see whether something could be worked out between them. Zapf responded with a visit in November 1965. Harald Peter, a former student of Georg Trump in Munich and director of Hallmark's new book department, met Zapf at the airport and drove him to the company's guest apartment situated on top of the headquarters building. The penthouse was designed in 1961 by Santa Fe architect Alexander Girard to receive and accommo-

Harald, who also studied with Herbert Post, started at Hallmark in 1961, the year the Berlin Wall was built.

date dealers and guests. Its eclectic interior featured such furnishings as a specially-designed wool carpet made in Morocco, a white Formica television and record player that disappeared into the wall when not in use, a wall-hung brass fireplace, and a forty-foot-long display case featuring part of Hallmark's antique card collection. Hermann enjoyed the apartment, recalling years later the "many happy times" spent there during his visits. Eventually, he would even use one of the whimsical ceramic objects Girard set around the apartment as a prop in the film, *The Art of Hermann Zapf.* According to Harald, the penthouse was where "many of the plans took shape"[12] regarding Hermann's contributions to the company.

Top and overleaf: Interior shots of the Hallmark penthouse (ca. 1961)

Right: Pete Seymour, who developed the outline for *The Art of Hermann Zapf,* and eventually followed Harald Peter as director of the book department, chatting with Ogden Nash in the penthouse

Points for discussion had been prepared in advance of Zapf's visit and included establishing a training program for lettering artists; giving lectures on typography, type, and calligraphic design; reviewing lettering on greeting cards and company typography; producing a film about calligraphy and/or typography—the proposal of which, according to Gordon, was met with some enthusiasm by Hermann, who already had been considering such an idea—and finally, hosting research trips to Europe. Designing type for Hallmark was not on the agenda.

A few months after Hermann's initial meeting with Peter, Archenhold, Lee, and Gordon, an agreement was made. Gordon was designated to coordinate Zapf's contacts, arrangements, and assignments (adding to his already considerable responsibilities) and recalls, "All of us involved were in accord and pleased with this new development for Hallmark…even Mr. Hall."[13]

Hermann's first entry in the penthouse guestbook, in which he shares a page with President Dwight D. Eisenhower

Calligraphy

ABC

Making the Movie

One of the first projects pursued was the development of the film, *The Art of Hermann Zapf,* produced during Zapf's first official visit as a consultant in mid-April 1966. This film and three separate exhibitions featuring various aspects of his work were made available to interested parties in an effort, as an accompanying brochure explained, "to stimulate interest, enthusiasm, and appreciation in the fields of typography, calligraphy, and type design."[1] This supportive gesture, more commonly reserved by corporations for the "fine arts," seems remarkable today.

The concept for the film was Harald Peter's. The script's outline was provided by Peter Seymour, a Hallmark writer with Hollywood ties, who eventually succeeded Harald as director of the book department. Hallmark editor and future Pulitzer Prize winner Richard Rhodes edited the script, and Noel Gordon acted as the film's production manager. Gordon, who can be seen in the film with Zapf, remembers that "Hermann was an inspiration to be around and to work with, day and night. Ideas seem to flow nonstop from his inventive mind."[2]

Peter Seymour is from a theatrical family that goes back to the eighteenth century. His aunt, Anne Seymour, was a busy actress on radio, stage, and screen.

Rhodes received the Pulitzer Prize in 1988 for The Making of the Atomic Bomb.

One of the most dramatic sequences in the movie was particularly challenging for Zapf, as he explains in *About Alphabets* (1970):

> Our cameraman came from Hawaii. He was used to big outdoor scenes with professional models. It was not easy—but a bottle of whiskey helped—to persuade him to shoot only my hands and letters, but finally the idea of the so-called "frog views" won him over: pictures taken through an Astralon-coated glass plate. On this slippery surface I had to write with a broad-edged pen, at midnight, with unpleasantly strong, hot camera lights trained on my neck, and so to design beautiful letters whose ink dried directly as the pen touched the Astralon sheet. Really not an easy job.[3]

Indeed, Gordon recalls that the filmmaking got increasingly complex the further into it they ventured, but "somehow, with many late nights, little sleep, many hours of editing, and practically living in the building, we managed to complete our film, with which we were all pleased."[4]

Influence of Movie: Recruitment and Public Relations

As Pete Seymour saw it, the film's purpose was to sell the art of lettering as "interesting, creative,... challenging, rewarding,... artistic, and very much alive today."[5] It certainly accomplished that, helping raise the standard of fine lettering used at Hallmark and serving, in part, as a recruiting tool for hiring promising lettering artists for the next decade and more. Sumner Stone, a calligrapher and future type designer who started at Hallmark in 1969, remembers:

Stone left Hallmark in 1972, eventually becoming the first director of type design at Adobe Systems and laying a foundation of excellence in that department that has continued ever since.

> The Zapf film was the reason I came to Hallmark. I saw it during the last class that Lloyd Reynolds taught at Reed College.... It was my first formal calligraphy class, although I had started doing calligraphy about a year and a half earlier with the help of friends who had already studied with him. I was already serious by the time I took the class. The film blew me away. I spent the fall making a portfolio to send to Hallmark to apply for a job. It was all about seeing and being around Hermann. I also liked the idea of having a real job making letters.[6]

The movie was popular wherever book lovers and those interested in lettering and typography gathered. For example, Bill Jackson, designer, teacher, and proprietor of the 4 Ducks Press, stated

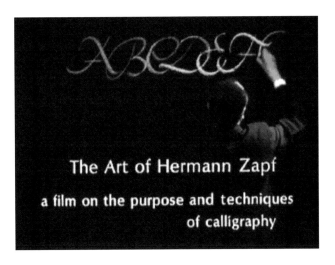

The Art of Hermann Zapf
a film on the purpose and techniques of calligraphy

Opposite: Part of the opening sequence of *The Art of Hermann Zapf*

Left to Right: Harald Peter, Hallmark photographer Fred Kautt, HZ sitting at table, cameraman Frank Robinson, and Noel Gordon, chatting on set

in the press's annual report of 1966 that he and the rest of the august Wichita Bibliophiles saw what must have been one of its first screenings at a dinner at the University of Kansas following a lecture there by esteemed California bookseller Jake Zeitlin. According to Susie Taylor, curator of the Richard Harrison Collection of Calligraphy & Lettering at the San Francisco Public Library, it was shown at the library in conjunction with the three Zapf exhibitions in 1977. And Phil Metzger, whose Crabgrass Press was Zapf's second home when he visited Kansas City, included it in a talk he gave to Chicago's Caxton Club in late September 1978.

Its use as a public relations tool grew when it was shown at a number of events in which Zapf participated, such as a session of the UNESCO meeting of the Association Typographique Internationale (ATypI) in Paris in 1967. That same year, *Publishers Weekly* noted in its April 3rd issue that the film was included in the evening's program when the New York Type Director's Club presented Zapf with its first gold medal.

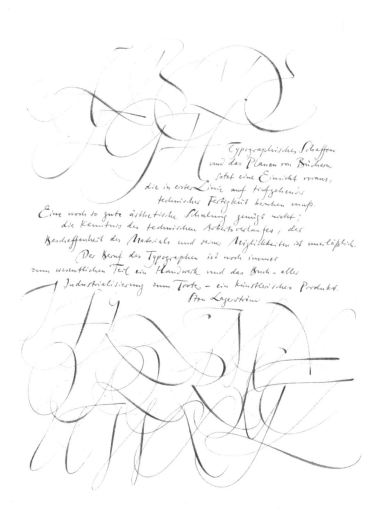

Original broadside rendered with
ballpoint pen included in the
exhibitions that traveled with the
film *The Art of Hermann Zapf*
(ca. 1966)

Douglas C.McMurtrie
We use the letters
of our alphabet every day
with the utmost ease and unconcern
taking them almost
as much for granted
as the air we breathe

We do not realize that each
of these letters is at our service today
only as the result of a long
and laboriously slow process of evolution
in the age-old art
of writing.

Le plus grand chef d'œuvre
de la littérature
n'est jamais qu'un alphabet
en désordre. Jean Cocteau

Das größte
ift das Alphabet,
denn alle Weisheit fteckt darin.
Aber nur der erkennt den Sinn, der's recht
zusammenzusetzen
verfteht.
Emanuel Geibel

Ἀρχὴ μεγίστη τοῦ βίου
Τὰ γράμματα.

Für Philip Hofer in Cambridge · geschrieben von Hermann Zapf Frankfurt am Main 1963

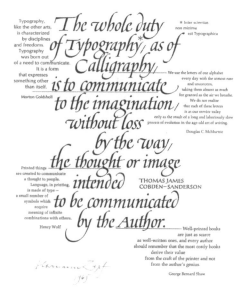

Typography,
like the other arts,
is characterized
by disciplines
and freedoms.
Typography
was born out
of a need to communicate.
It is a form
that expresses
something other
than itself.
Morton Goldsholl

The whole duty
of Typography*, as of
Calligraphy,
is to communicate
to the imagination,
without loss
by the way,
the thought or image
intended
to be communicated
by the Author.

* Inter scientias
non minima
est Typographica

We use the letters of our alphabet
every day with the utmost ease
and unconcern,
taking them almost as much
for granted as the air we breathe.
We do not realize
that each of these letters
is at our service today
only as the result of a long and laboriously slow
process of evolution in the age-old art of writing.

Douglas C. McMurtrie

Printed things —
are created to communicate
a thought to people.
Language, in printing,
is made of type —
a small number of
symbols which
acquire
meaning of infinite
combinations with others.
Henry Wolf

THOMAS JAMES
COBDEN–SANDERSON

Well-printed books
are just as scarce
as well-written ones, and every author
should remember that the most costly books
derive their value
from the craft of the printer and not
from the author's genius.
George Bernard Shaw

Printed broadsides
included in exhibitions
that traveled with the
film, the bottom one a
letterpress piece designed
for a talk HZ gave at
UCLA in 1958

17

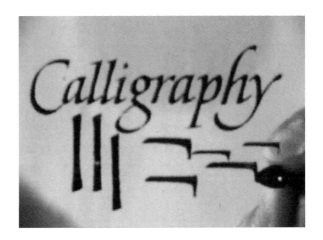

Still illustrating HZ's pen-twisting and pressure technique

Printing News, acknowledged as "the authoritative weekly newspaper of the printing industry,"[7] reported in 1969 that the movie was part of an exhibition of Zapf's work arranged by Hallmark at Gallery 303 in New York, a notable venue for Hallmark's name to be associated with. The gallery was opened by Dr. Robert L. Leslie in association with The Composing Room, one of the city's best typesetting shops, which he founded with Sol Cantor in 1927. Celebrated art director Gene Federico once described Gallery 303 as "probably the only place in New York City where young designers came into contact with the freshest work being done in graphics and advertising. European émigrés were shown regularly. Its contribution to the graphic design community was inestimable."[8] In 1965, Leslie initiated the popular "Heritage of the Graphic Arts"

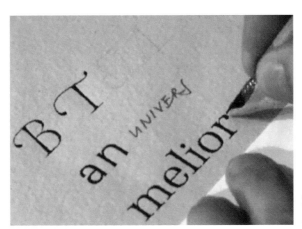

Still illustrating how the broad-edged pen can be used to indicate typefaces

lecture series, bringing speakers into the gallery from around the world. Zapf spoke for the first time in the series just a few months before the Hallmark exhibition opened.

New Medium for Instruction and Inspiration

An important aspect of the film was the demonstration of Zapf's method of pen manipulation and his now well-known technique of applying pressure to various parts of a letter when rendering it—something he likened to playing the piano. Before the film's release, few students or professionals would have had the opportunity to see him demonstrate this. It had been more than fifteen years since he conducted his night classes at the Werkkunstschule in Offenbach-am-Main. It would be another dozen years before he would initiate his popular classes at Rochester Institute of Technology (RIT) when he was named the Melbert B. Cary Jr. Professor of Graphic Arts, (replacing the esteemed Alexander Lawson, who had retired after thirty years.)

Beyond its use for instruction, the movie offered Zapf a different medium to express a few of his thoughts on the purpose of calligraphy. Zapf's reputation as a calligrapher was unparalleled,

In 1960, Zapf taught a six-week seminar at Carnegie-Mellon in book design, type design and calligraphy.

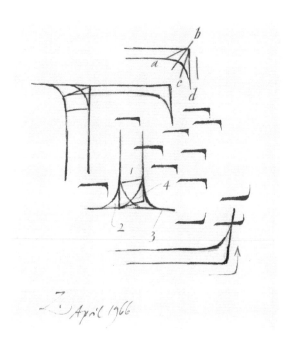

Original art from the film showing stroke sequence and pen-twisting methods to form serifs

Still from the film showing Hermann's pressure technique, something he likened to playing the piano

Opposite page: Masthead for *The Committee for Italic Handwriting Newsletter* by Raymond F. DaBoll

but up to this point he had not yet published anything of a personal nature on the subject. His notes in *Feder und Stichel* (1950), a virtuosic display of alphabets and pages of calligraphy, are historical in content. And most of his lectures and other writings, while acknowledging the importance of calligraphy as a foundation for type design, concentrated on type and typography and how they would be affected by emerging technologies (a recurring theme throughout his career). Even in his autobiography *About Alphabets*, there is scant reference to calligraphy, staying true to its subtitle, "Some Marginal Notes on Type Design." In effect, the film was Zapf's first opportunity to bring to a wide audience something of his philosophy regarding the subject until 1978, when he touched upon it a little more intimately in the article "The Brotherhood of Calligraphers," his contribution to *With Respect...to RFD*, my tribute to calligrapher Raymond Franklin DaBoll.[9]

Others who contributed articles included: Edward M. Catich, Paul Standard, Heather Child, Egdon H. Margo, R. Hunter Middleton, Arnold Bank, and DeForrest Sackett.

Zapf reprinted the article in 1987 in Herman Zapf & His Design Philosophy.

Part of a Renaissance

The film is notable for helping stir public interest in calligraphy and, along with other events and activities in the early and mid-1960s, for helping pave the way for the emergence in the 1970s of numerous organizations in the United States dedicated to all aspects of the lettering arts. Earlier in the decade there had been two major exhibitions featuring calligraphy and handwriting, both of them held in Baltimore. The first, "Calligraphy and Handwriting in America," was presented in 1961. The second and more comprehensive was "Two Thousand Years of Calligraphy" in 1965, which took the space of three museums to accommodate.

The Committee for Italic Handwriting, active for most of the decade, was an organization dedicated to promoting the teaching of italic handwriting (and getting it taught as an alternative handwriting method in elementary and secondary schools). The committee had the support of teachers like Lloyd Reynolds and Paul Standard, professionals such as James Hayes and Ray DaBoll, as well as a number of dedicated amateurs. The group published an informative newsletter under the auspices of RIT's School of Printing until a lack of funding caused its demise around 1968. Soon after, a Western American Branch of (London's) Society for Italic Handwriting was formed, spearheaded by Reynolds.

In 1967, writer Paul Vandervoort did his part to promote calligraphic letterforms to the sign industry when he initiated his long-running series of articles on calligraphers in *Signs of the Times* magazine, beginning with the work of Maury Nemoy and eventually including many of the major names of the day. A few years later, *American Artist* ran an article on British calligrapher Donald Jackson, well-known as "The Queen's Scribe"—a label both accurate and misleading.[10] In what could be described as a triumph of

The Committee for Italic Handwriting
SPRING & SUMMER Newsletter 1961
Sponsored by ROCHESTER INSTITUTE OF TECHNOLOGY, 65 Plymouth Ave, S. Rochester 8, New York
Published and distributed without charge to persons in the United States interested in Italic handwriting

craftsmanship and charisma, Jackson's subsequent workshops and lectures created enough enthusiasm throughout the United States to prompt an essentially amateur base to form into clubs to study calligraphy and related arts, eventually leading to the organization of annual conferences. Those in the larger cities had the benefit of local professionals for additional guidance and inspiration. Nemoy, for instance, accepted the role of mentor to the

We use the letters of our alphabet every day with the utmost ease and unconcern, taking them almost as much for granted as the air we breathe. We do not realize that each of these letters is at our service today only as the result of a long & laboriously slow process of evolution in the age-old art of writing.

ABC DEFGHI JKLM NOPQ RSTUVW XYZ

Douglas C. McMurtrie

Printed broadside from
the exhibitions that
traveled with the film,
The Art of Hermann Zapf

Society for Calligraphy in Los Angeles. The 1960s back-to-basics craft culture played its part in setting the stage as well, a point reinforced by the *Wall Street Journal* in 1978 when it ran a front-page article declaring calligraphy to be "hotter than macramé."[11] The same article reported that some thirty-five calligraphy societies were then in existence.

Today, concern is occasionally expressed about the "digital threat" to calligraphy, the profusion of informal typestyles over the past twenty-five years cited as the main argument. But long-term negative effects are unlikely. Since its revival at the beginning of the twentieth century by Edward Johnston and his followers, the craft has proven to be resilient, as Beatrice Warde pointed out in her review in the *London Times* of the 1965 Baltimore exhibition:

> The art of calligraphy has twice been killed stone dead by a mechanical invention and has twice found a new life and a new set

of justifications. As an industry for copying of texts, it was destroyed by the printing press. As an essential tool of commerce and finance, and as an evidence of gentility, it flourished for three centuries and was strangled by the typewriter. In its third and present life, it stands with the fine arts, safe from any further technological threat.[12]

What digital technology and the desktop computer have done is to democratize the equally esoteric world of type design, creating in its wake a frenzy for sources from which to mine. Not since the Renaissance have letterforms been so thoroughly analyzed, dissected, and discussed by so many people. Past masters such as W. A. Dwiggins, Oswald Cooper, Charles Bluemlein, and Oldrich Menhart, long considered passé by the postmodern design community, might be surprised to learn how thoroughly their work is being researched (and in some cases digitized and turned into fonts).

However, the increased interest in letterpress printing and other book arts in schools today might lead to more lettering classes.

Even with this increased scrutiny, few design schools and university art programs offer students in-depth exposure to traditional letter making. As a result, the future of such work may be primarily in the hands of organizations formed in the 1970s, stimulated by such events as the making of *The Art of Hermann Zapf* a decade earlier.

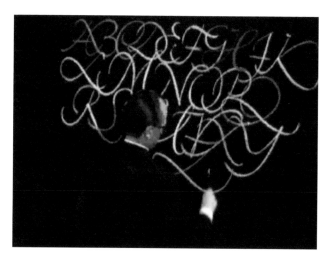

Part of the ending sequence from
The Art of Hermann Zapf

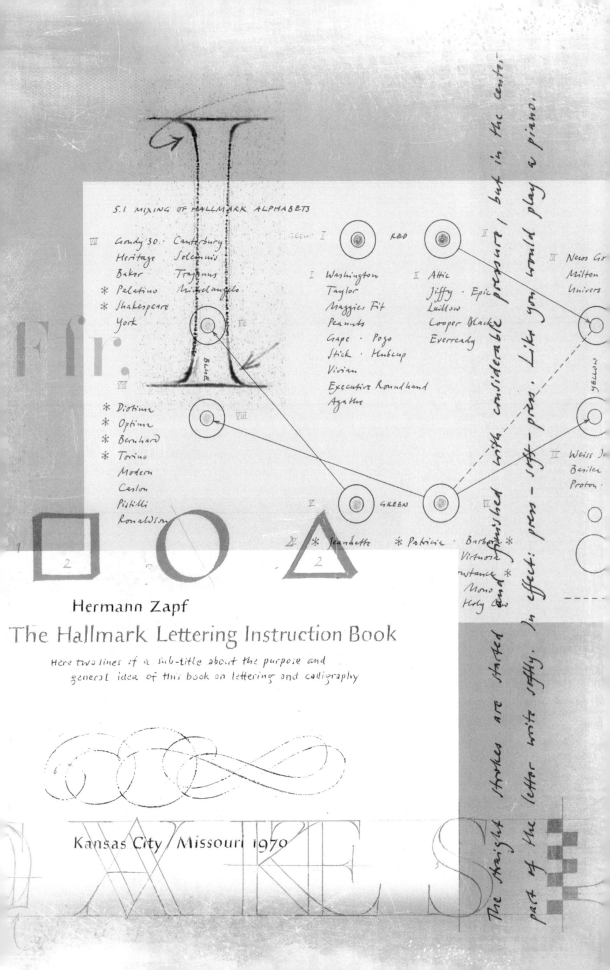

5.1 MIXING OF HALLMARK ALPHABETS

VI Gaudy 30 · Canterbury
    Heritage   Solemnis
    Baker   Trajanus
*   Palatino   Michelangelo
*   Shakespeare
    York

* Diotima
* Optima
* Bernhard
* Torino
  Modern
  Caslon
  Pistilli
  Ronaldson

Group I   RED   II

I   Washington   II Attic
    Taylor   Jiffy · Epic
    Maggies Fit   Ludlow
    Peanuts   Cooper Black
    Grape · Pogo   Everready
    Stick · Hubcup
    Vivian
    Executive Roundhand
    Agathe

III News Gr
     Milton
     Univers

IV   Weiss J
     Basilea
     Proton

GREEN

X * Jeandette   * Patricia Barbara
                              Victoria
                   onstance *
                     Mono
                     Holy Co

Hermann Zapf
The Hallmark Lettering Instruction Book

Here two lines of a sub-title about the purpose and
general idea of this book on lettering and calligraphy

Kansas City / Missouri 1970

The straight strokes are started and finished with considerable pressure, but in the center, but in the center, like you would play a piano. In effect: press – soft – press. Like you would play a piano.

part of the letter with softly.

THREE: THE LETTERING MANUAL

The Hallmark Lettering Instruction Book, commonly referred to as the "manual," was written at Hallmark's request in conjunction with a series of seminars Zapf conducted for the lettering staff in 1968. This project allowed Hermann to set down his thoughts and what he had learned over more than twenty-five years in the business of lettering and calligraphy. Written with the professional in mind and with the stated aim of doing better lettering in less time, it contained, as he writes in the 1970 edition of *About Alphabets*, "new training methods, unusual tricks, and time-saving techniques."[1] Zapf was pragmatic in his approach, stating early in the Introduction, "As you gain confidence in your ability, your own personality will struggle against the style of the teacher."[2] He concludes with the sentiment of all thoughtful teachers, "Learn what is there to learn, then go your own way." Although it was never published, the manual was a constant source of inspiration for an aspiring designer and lettering artist.

Some of the information in the manual pertaining to the use of the broad-edged pen is necessarily similar to what eventually appeared in an instruction booklet Zapf prepared for Rotring Ltd.,[3] the German pen manufacturer, in 1985. The Rotring booklet delves deeper into historical calligraphic hands than the Hallmark manual, offering exemplars for roman, italic, textura, rotunda and uncial, as well as a model for italic handwriting. The Hallmark manual goes beyond broad-edged pen calligraphy—covering only roman, italic, and something Zapf calls "The Flat Principles of the Broad Pen" (a technique for rendering Bodoniesque forms)—but includes instruction in such things as how to draw script alphabets for photocomposition using prints of repeated structural elements, a method for drawing flourishes for reproduction using a ballpoint pen, and the "clip and tip" technique, where pre-printed or freshly drawn swashes and flourishes are attached to a piece of lettering or type.

In the Hallmark manual, Zapf advises using one's handwriting as a way to develop personality in calligraphic work, but cautions: "Weak characters or carelessness in general should not be

The Rotring booklet, Creative Calligraphy; Instructions and Alphabets, was published in four language editions: English, German, French, and Spanish.

sized pen the ink must be more thicker than for a larger pen which we use now for the first exercises in capital letters (→ 3.4).

The angle determines very much the weight of the stroke

a

Position of the pen as you can see it in old manuscripts

b

A few experiments in using the same pen in different angles will illustrate this clearly to you. Compare the two possibilities as it is shown under a and c

c

The pen should be held itself not the pen-holder for maximum control, firmly, but not

confused with individuality."[4] He also provides a diagram with his suggestions for mixing some of the typefaces then available at Hallmark, as well as a few tips on typography regarding such things as the staggering of lines. The principles in the manual became so infused into the practice of some members of the Lettering Department that later artists absorbed them without really knowing the original source of inspiration, thus furthering Hermann's influence on Hallmark's products.

A few artists hired after Zapf's tenure at Hallmark were also sent to his summer classes at RIT.

Naturally, as artists left the company, the influence of Zapf and his manual went with them. Sumner Stone was particularly successful at synthesizing what he learned from Lloyd Reynolds with Zapf's teachings:

> Hermann had a giant impact on me. I tried very hard to learn his techniques—using pressure with the metal-edged pen and also the amazing ballpoint gymnastics. I recall doing exercises with both the ballpoint and an edged pencil on clay-coated proofing paper. I really wanted to be able to make letters the way he did. I thought they were beautiful, so subtle and sophisticated, relative to most of the calligraphy I had been exposed to up to that point.[5]

Bill's foundation was provided by Catich, but his natural flair blossomed when exposed to Zapf's influence.

In the early 1980s, when Hallmark's lettering department was managed by Bill LaFever, a fine calligrapher and former student of Father Edward M. Catich at St. Ambrose College, he asked me to revisit the possibility of publishing the manual. Hermann and I discussed it at length. I suggested that we treat it as a historical document and reproduce it in facsimile with his original handwritten text, perhaps with a new introduction by him. There were

Study the following optical effects for they are important to understand the structure of the capital letters. Between geometrical adjustments and optical illusions are differences which you must know:

The horizontal lines looking more heavier than the vertical lines

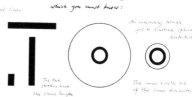

An interesting trouble spot to illustrate optical distortion

The two strokes have the same length

The inner circles are of the same diameter

The condensed E looks larger than the expanded form.

To satisfy the eye the bar must be in the optical center that means a little above the geometrical center (E too high, H is ok).

An important optical illusion for lettering: The circle and the triangle only touches the lines. They will seem smaller than the square. In capital letters therefore round and pointed letters have to be extended a bit above or below the guide lines

3.72 DIAGRAMS AND PROPORTIONS OF CAPITAL LETTERS

also for R P K S   1/10 for X Y and Z   optically a square   M and W is optically 1/3 wider than a square

MODUL 1:10

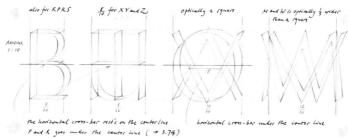

the horizontal cross-bar rests on the center line
P and R goes under the centre line (→ 3.74)

horizontal cross-bar under the center line

Notice the upper loop of the B is smaller than the lower one. The horizontal stroke of E is slightly longer than the two upper strokes.

The round curve of U tapers to a point to touch the right vertical main stroke. Another form of U is this: U but not easy for a beginner.

The round letters are only an optical circle, they project slightly below and above the guide lines. Also the points of A and V.

This W is made of two condensed V's. The legs of the M are slightly splayed from the vertical, they are not parallel with the V in the center.

Opposite: Diagram showing correct angle of the pen to the surface

Top: Optical considerations pertaining to lettering

Bottom: Diagrams showing proportions of majuscule letters

Top: Making capital letters with serifs
using the broad-edged pen

Bottom: Illustration showing a unit system
as a guide in joining script letters

28

Design very carefully the basic structure
elements of the alphabet (1 or 1½ inch
high). Make a photograph and as many
prints you need for your alphabet.
Paste the different pieces together (→ 4.1),
add the other parts and make a new
photograph.

An alphabet of English Script built up by the
above elements

Before developing your own style you must know the elementary principles.

2.15   CAPITAL SCRIPT LETTERS

A new interpretation of an idea of R. Peale (1778-1860), an early American writing master.
(He was the painter of the George Washington portrait on U.S. Dollar bills).
Use the oval as a basic unit and draw your letters with a ball-point within one or two of
these elements. (→ 2.6).

The forms must have grace and looking not battered or bend out of shape. Each malformation
will reduce the whole impression and elegance of your design.

Top: Developing alphabets using repeated
structural elements

Bottom: Method of using the oval as a basic
unit for rendering script forms

practical reasons for this option. Because of the subtlety of his original art (he used a combination of graphite, black ink, red and blue ballpoint, and light blue colored pencil to get his points across), compromises would have had to be made for printing. In addition, some of the materials he mentioned in the text were no longer available, such as Reylon proofing paper acquired from the Ludlow Typograph Company and a mechanical carpenter's pencil manufactured by A. W. Faber-Castell. Addressing both factors would have required Hermann to spend considerably more time and effort on the project. But he disagreed with my holographic idea, feeling that the manual should be published as it was originally intended, with updated information and, this time, set in Crown Roman as opposed to the Optima look-alike that was used in the rough typeset mock-up prepared in 1970. Alas, a poorly-timed reorganization in the creative division stopped any further work on the project.

There's a note in the Hallmark archives stating that, if ever published, the manual should be typeset rather than reproduced in facsimile.

In 1976, Zapf showed photocopied pages of his original in the exhibition "Gutenbergs Kunst im deutschen Buch" at the Gutenberg Museum and reproduced two pages from it with a combination of typeset and handwritten text in *Hermann Zapf: Ein Arbeitsbericht*, distributed in 1984 to members of the Maxmilian-Gesellschaft, an association of bibliophiles. The same two pages appeared in *Hermann Zapf & His Design Philosophy*, published in 1987 by the Society of Typographic Arts, and *Sammlung Hermann Zapf*, a catalog from 1993 recording the Zapf collection housed in the Herzog August Bibliothek in Wolfenbüttel.

Diagram for italic minuscules

Top: Rendering "clip and tip" flourishes from warm-up exercises

Bottom: Showing the possibilities of tools such as a fountain pen and carpenter's pencil to help transform one's normal handwriting into calligraphic letterforms

nianibnicnidnienifnignihnünijniknilnim

ninnionipniqnirnisnitniunivniwnixniyniz

new design

too close

Pack my box with five dizen red liquor jugs

too narrow (new form)

the quick brown fox jumps over the lazy grey d

change design

ipniqnirnisnitniunivniwnixniyniz

ABCDEF
GHIJK
LMNOPQ
RSTU
VWX

this design
belongs to
small letter

S

M

n

ß

FOUR: TYPOGRAPHIC TRANSITION

The beginning of the Hallmark/Zapf relationship roughly coincided with the beginning of the corporation's in-house photocomposition service, as well as the inception of its own font development group—the Alphabet Group, as it was originally called. The latter was led for most of its first thirty years by Myron McVay, a first-rate typographer and lettering artist.

Hermann preferred the term alphabet *for designs for photocomposition. I have freely interchanged,* alphabet, typeface, *and* font *in this book.*

The precursor to this group began in 1964 when McVay, having already begun drawing alphabets for Hallmark's Filmotype machine, recruited Jim Parkinson from the ranks and the two of them began drawing alphabets for the PhotoTypositor (Visual Graphics Corp.). Parkinson left Hallmark in 1969 and became successful designing fonts, logos, and mastheads for magazines and newspapers around the world. His exposure to Zapf while at Hallmark was sporadic, yet he feels that Zapf had a big influence on the general direction of his working life, even though it may not be reflected in his lettering:

> Hermann was the first type designer I ever met and I was struck by the fact that a guy could make a living designing alphabets outside of Hallmark. He was very formal and reserved and kind of elegant, but he had a good sense of humor and was quick to smile. I learned a lot of things from him, some specific, some secondhand (through Myron), and some big stuff, all-encompassing and vague...like 'You can make a living doing this. See?'[1]

McVay, as the head of the Alphabet Group, spent a good deal of time with Zapf during his annual visits. He felt that Hermann influenced him to loosen up and allow more irregularity when designing casual alphabets, a trait that would grow over the years. Most of the broad-edged pen lettering that he executed for product, largely inspired by Zapf models, tended toward the semiformal. His range was considerable and Hermann had high regard for his ability: "He was so good to work with and very accommodating. Whatever I asked, Myron could do. No problem."[2] McVay, who retired in 1997 after 37 years, was unique at Hallmark in that he had the capacity and desire to understand the technical as well as the aesthetic aspects of making type, though his recollection is that "we were learning as we went along."[3] Before graduating from Colorado State University, McVay had attended Art Center for three years where he had studied lettering with Mort Leach's

Merry Christmas

young colleague, Doyald Young. He also brought practical job-printing experience with him to Hallmark, having worked in a printing shop in between colleges.

Although his passion for letterforms was occasionally disguised by a faculty to appear unconcerned, McVay was a teacher at heart, willing to share with those ready to learn. According to Parkinson, "Myron was the person who taught me more about lettering and type design than anybody else."[4] Indeed, McVay's contribution to Hallmark's lettering, typography, and font development was profound, and the company was particularly fortunate that he was there to guide the Alphabet Group from the

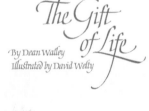

By Dean Walley
Illustrated by David Welty

❧ Hallmark Crown Editions

34

How like a mother is the rich earth
that nurtures a sapling in springtime.....
....and takes the cast-off
leaves in autumn.....
only to return them, green and filled with life,
in an endless cycle of love ....

For unto us a child is born, unto us a son is given,
And his name shall be called... Prince of Peace.
—ISAIAH

Look
To This
Day

Swanson's
on the plaza

Lettering by Myron McVay from the '60s
and '70s, including a brush written logo for
a tony women's department store once
owned by Hallmark

beginning—it was, as Harald Peter recalls, "thanks to Myron…
and his superior knowledge, [that] the type design program for
Hallmark became [a] reality."[5]

Hallmark's decision to establish an in-house photocomposition department was a matter of efficiency. McVay recalls that
when he started with the company in 1961, as much as 90 percent
of the work was being hand lettered. To save time, it was decided
that a larger portion of the work could be typeset. This would
allow artists more time to concentrate on designing, and on what
remained to be rendered by hand—most often the caption and
the tag. According to Archenhold, Zapf had input on this decision, which reduced the amount of work enormously. Certainly,
it was in keeping with Hermann's often-stated belief (given also
in the Hallmark film) that "tradition and progress must be logi-
cally united."

*The tag is a kind
of summation that
follows the inside
sentiment, for
instance: "With
Love on Your
Anniversary."*

The typesetting equipment that Hallmark chose was manufactured by Alphatype in Skokie, Illinois, and if buying it was considered to be an economic necessity, the formation of the Alphabet Group was equally important because it addressed a perceived
aesthetic necessity. McVay stated in an in-house interview thirty
years later, "We had to do that…because whatever machine you
bought, the typefaces that were on that machine were absolutely
unique to it."[6] And those typefaces were generally uneven in quality. As one industry expert observed: "Few, if any, of these early
libraries featured high-quality designs. A newspaper would demand that the new phototypesetter match the fonts already in use
by its hot-metal system. Advertising agencies would demand the
latest sans serif in vogue."[7] As a result, the Alphabet Group's main
function was to develop typefaces that exhibited the kind of variety and distinction considered important for Hallmark products.

What began as a bid for efficiency and as a solution for aesthetic shortcomings eventually became a point of differentiation
in the marketplace for Hallmark, a serendipitous result not fully
appreciated by the company at first. It can be argued that the
many casual designs the group developed during this time, especially those based on handwriting, were a unique contribution to
the world of type design. But because of their proprietary status,

36

Hallmark alphabets were largely unknown in the type industry, although a few were appropriated even when that task was still relatively expensive to accomplish.

The Zapf Alphabets

Remarkably, designing exclusive alphabets for Hallmark was not on the list of things to be discussed during Zapf's first visit in November 1965. But the sense of it was soon realized, and by the following January, when Noel Gordon wrote Hermann confirming Hallmark's interest in having him work with the company, he included the following as one of several things Hermann might consider: "Propose and design a calligraphic style or styles to be put on our Typositor machine for exclusive use on Hallmark products."[8] Eventually, according to Hermann, the question "Do you have some new ideas for types?" became a familiar refrain.[9] Today the alphabets are the most obvious reminders of his contribution to the company, although their inclusion in Hallmark's vast font library doesn't begin to reveal the inspiration they provided to members of the lettering staff when they were first introduced.

The timing was advantageous for both parties. By then, Zapf, in response to the widespread plagiarism of his work, had largely withdrawn from developing new commercial type designs. Consequently, twelve of the fourteen original alphabets he designed during this period, and the only one designed by his wife, Gudrun Zapf von Hesse, were for Hallmark. The company's explorations into the realm of photocomposition provided Hermann with a unique opportunity to explore mainly calligraphic directions. After more than twenty-five years of designing type informed by his calligraphy, including some of the most important typefaces of the twentieth century, he was in a position to fully exploit the broad-edged pen as a more determined partner with technology.

Designing for photocomposition was not without its technical challenges—for example, the 18-unit grid into which all characters had to fit. While the drawings had to be more precise than drawings for metal type founding (because in metal type founding, inaccuracies were corrected in the final cutting by hand or machine), designing for photocomposition allowed more flexibility and the possibility of refinements such as thinner hairlines. Not surprisingly, Zapf's emphasis on traditional calligraphic forms gave the Hallmark collection a classical and decidedly bookish feel, and, indeed, the alphabets saw considerable use in Hallmark books as well as on greeting cards. McVay surmises that Harald Peter was initially interested in developing a house style for the book line by having a distinguished collection of proprietary alphabets available. Whether this was his intent or not, it was Harald's good fortune to have Hermann Zapf available to provide such designs, and it is clear from existing correspondence and written comments on early alphabet tests that Harald had some input. However, Hermann was not heavily directed for specific design approaches. This unusual lack of restraint paid off splendidly for Hallmark with a new typographic direction for its products. By holding true to his aesthetic, Zapf avoided the mistakes of many designers whose efforts, due largely to preconceived notions about the social expression industry, often result in caricature.

This is not to say that every type design Hermann proposed was accepted. At least two submitted late in his tenure were rejected — most likely cost-saving decisions.

Accurately documenting the alphabets that Hermann and Gudrun designed for Hallmark provides a challenge for the researcher. One reason is because of the confusion over the names given to them (and in at least one instance, a discrepancy in the dating of a design). For example, Zapf assigned a totally different name to an alphabet that was an extension to one he had executed a few years earlier. Adding to the confusion was the notion of giving names to specific combinations of a few of the typefaces he and Gudrun designed. Although technically part of their oeuvre, these combinations were never released as separately-named designs.

Naming a typeface, as Hermann suggests in *About Alphabets*, can be a challenging experience in itself: "Sales considerations being generally decisive when a type is named, the child occasionally acquires a rather sonorous but fundamentally unsuitable name."[10] He tells us that Melior was first called Columbia, then

Shirley Temple and Shirley Temple Black

Opposite: I Dunno and I Dunno Fat Face

SHIRLEYTEMPLE**BLACK**

38

Tempora. He preferred Medici for what became Palatino and Neu Antiqua instead of Optima, which he considered a bit pretentious. At Hallmark, where there are no such marketing concerns when it comes to naming fonts (since they are proprietary), humorous or facetious names have long been a tradition. For example, in the mid-1960s, Jim Parkinson named an outlined alphabet for iconic child actress of the 1930s Shirley Temple and then

abcdeefffighijklmnopqrstuvwxyyz
AABCDDEFGHIJKLMNOPQRSSTUVWXYZ

abcdefffifghijklmnooopqrstuvwxyz
AAABCDEFGHiJKLMNOPQRSTUVWXYZ

released a filled-in version called Shirley Temple Black, her married name. He called a couple of other early designs I Dunno and I Dunno Fatface, hoping that one day an art director (or anyone else) would ask, "What typeface is that?" In fact, that was the design he was developing when he first met Zapf, "Myron suggested I show Hermann what I was working on. It was a little embarrassing to show Hermann Zapf my drawings for I Dunno Fatface. But Hermann was very composed and polite and managed to look at I Dunno without choking or bursting out laughing."[11]

At least half of the alphabets Zapf designed for Hallmark have names in some way related to the company, e.g., Jeannette, Hallmark Uncial, Hallmark Textura, Crown Roman, and Missouri, an approach that Parkinson found useful in his work after he left the company. "I learned from Hermann that naming a custom typeface after the client is a great idea. If the design carries their name, they seem to be much more interested and receptive to it than they would otherwise. All of my custom fonts have been named after the clients. It works."[12] An inadvertent lesson from Hermann, no doubt, but effective nonetheless.

*   *   *

Jeannette—1966/67

Dates following the name of each alphabet correspond with those appearing in Hermann Zapf & His Design Philosophy.

The first Hallmark alphabet Zapf designed was Jeannette, a connected script inspired by Jeannette Lee's handwriting but drawn with the influence of a broad-edged pen. It had its origin at a Sunday brunch at Mr. Hall's farm. Lee recalls that "the subject of handwriting came up, and Hermann and the rest of us all sat around the table and began to write."[13]

During the course of its development, Zapf asked McVay to provide additional examples of "typical" American handwriting to draw upon. In addition to the basic font, Zapf designed a number of ligatured characters and alternate caps. It was the first of dozens of alphabets at Hallmark based on actual handwriting as opposed to lettering, designed to look casual. Its rough texture, which Hermann told me initially concerned Hallmark's engravers because they were afraid it would reflect badly on their craftsmanship, influenced future alphabet designs at Hallmark as well as some of the lettering done by the staff.

The only real valuable thing is intuition.

ALBERT EINSTEIN

1 2 3 4 5 6 7 8 9 + 0

This page and opposite: HZ's studies and examples of Jeannette Lee's handwriting

40

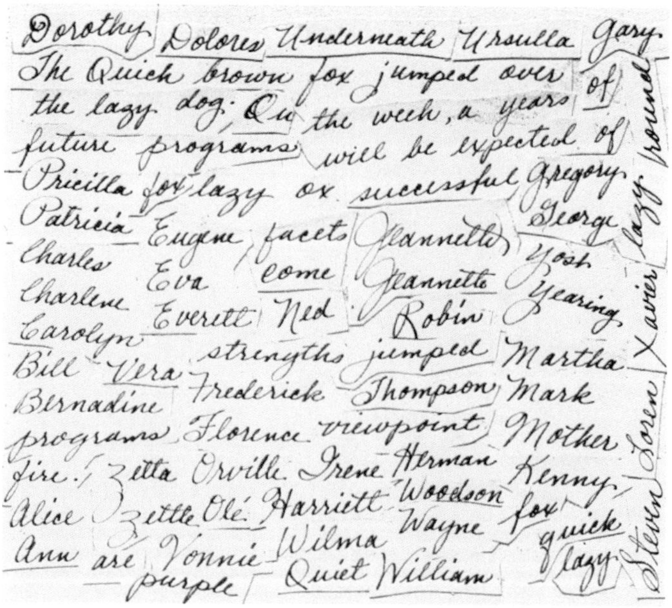

Dorothy Dolores Underneath Ursulla Gary.
The Quick brown fox jumped over
the lazy dog. Qu the week, a years of
future programs will be expected of
Pricilla fox lazy ox successful Gregory.
Patricia Eugene facets Jeannette George
Charles Eva come Jeannette Yost
Charlene Eva Everett Ned Robin Yearing
Carolyn strengths jumped Martha
Bill Vera Frederick Thompson Mark
Bernadine Florence viewpoint Mother
programs Florence Irene Herman Kenny
fire. Zetta Orville Irene Herman fox
Alice Zette Olé. Harriett Woodson fox
Ann are Vonnie Wilma Wayne quick
purple Quiet William lazy

Steven Soren Xavier lazy pronoun

A a A B B C Ch D D E E 7

a a b c c & d d e e e f f f g h i

F F G G G H H I J J J K

j k k l l m m m n w n o o p r r r

K L L L M M M N N O P

r s t u u v w w x x y y y y z

P Q R R R S S S S T Th U U

ch gs ll nd of pp qu ss tt &!?

V V V W W W W X Y Z Z

41

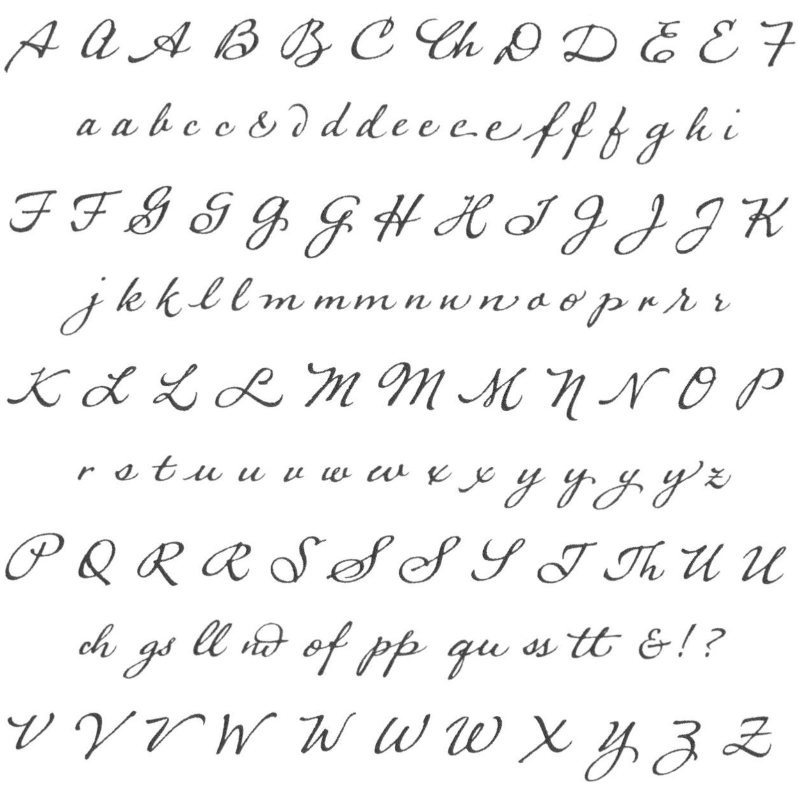

Firenze — 1967/72

Firenze, a contemporary chancery italic with swash caps and an alternate set of lowercase characters, signaled a major movement toward calligraphic lettering at Hallmark. The typographic look, especially on greeting cards, became more diverse when it was introduced. Used extensively on Hallmark products and still prevalent when I joined the company in late 1971, Firenze was treated by many there as an archetype for the italic form. Familiarity with the letterform occurred naturally as artists added their own swash strokes to the typeface, using the "clip and tip" method Hermann introduced in the lettering manual.

In 1972, Zapf added a companion set of capitals which he lists as Arno in *Hermann Zapf & His Design Philosophy*, acknowledging its Italian heritage. But on the final art submitted to Hallmark, he wrote "Hallmark Firenze Caps," which is what it was named when it was released. The serif treatment in these later caps was slightly different than in the original Firenze, suggesting more pronounced traces of the broad-edged pen (though his proposal for the font was drawn with a ballpoint pen).

abcdefghijklmnopqrstuvwxyz!?

1 2 3 4 5 6 7 8 9 0

& abcdefghijklmnopqrstuvwxyz

A A B C D E F G H I J K L M
N O P Q R S T U V W X Y Z

A B C D E F G H I J K L M N O
P Q R S T U V W X Y Z &

KANSAS CITY

MOTHER'S DAY

GIVE BOX 19

PARIS UNITED

FIRENZE CAPS

QU WINE ART

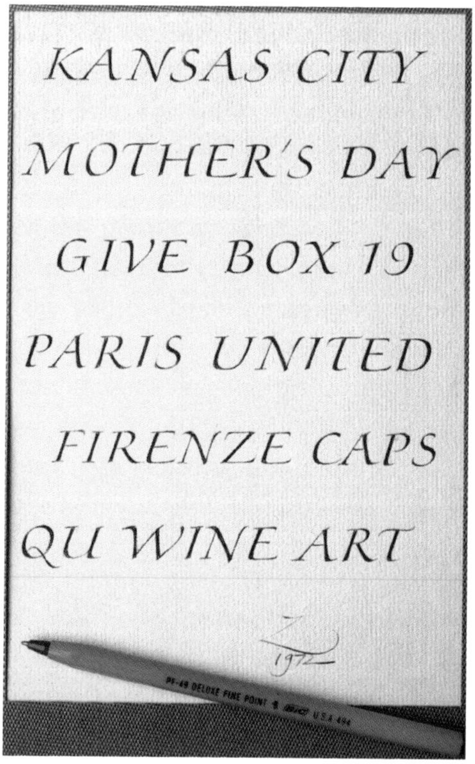

NATURE
does not hurry,
yet everything
is accomplished.

LAO TSE

Opposite: Study for Firenze

Left: Proposal for Firenze fit caps,
also known as Arno

43

In der still.zurückhaltenden/
edel.durchgebildeten/aufs tiefste
in jeder bewegung erfühlten schriftform
suchen wir uns und unser zeitgefühl.
auszudrücken

Rudolf Koch

ABCDEFGHIJ
KLMNOPQRST
UVWXYZ
W

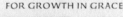

FOR GROWTH IN GRACE

GIVE PERFECTION TO
beginners/O Father/
give intelligence to
the little ones/give
aid to those who
are running their
course. Give sorrow
to the negligent/
give fervor of spirit
to the lukewarm.
Give to the perfect a
good consummation
for the sake of Christ Jesus our Lord. — Amen.

✠ St.Irenaeus/Bishop of Lyons/A.D. 130 – 202 ✠

Vergleich American Uncial
und Hallmark Uncial

GGG

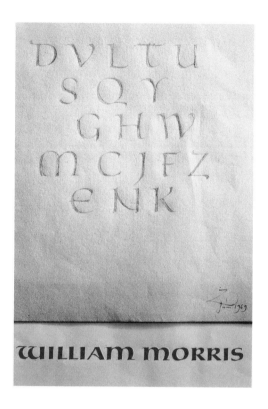

Studies for Hallmark Uncial

Opposite: HZ's calligraphy from *Pen and Graver*

Bottom: Studies for cap G on page set in Hammer Uncial (by Victor Hammer)

Right: Study from HZ's title calligraphy for his book on William Morris (1949)

Hallmark Uncial — 1968

Out of the more than 200 typefaces designed by Zapf, this alphabet is the only one based on the uncial form. There is a set of large caps and a companion set of small caps that can be used separately or in conjunction with one another. With the exception of the large capital E, the characteristic round uncial form is more strictly observed in the alternate letters for d, q, m, h, w, and n that he provided for the small cap alphabet than in either of the two main alphabets. In addition, the large caps were also intended to be mixed with the lowercase of Gudrun's Shakespeare alphabet, designed for Hallmark in the same year. This combination was dubbed Hallmark Charlemagne. When the uncial caps were combined with the textura alphabet Hermann completed in 1969, it was called Hallmark Stratford. He made numerous comparative studies with some of his older calligraphic pieces as well as with existing uncial typefaces.

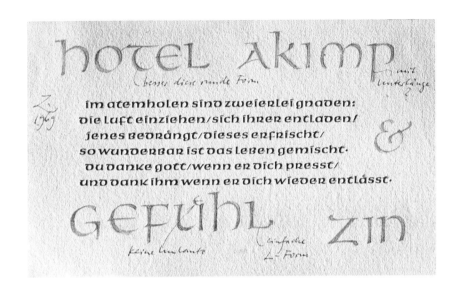

ART IS THE PROPER TASK OF LIFE.

FRIEDRICH NIETZSCHE

Studies for Hallmark Uncial

Top: Page set in Victor Hammer's Hammer Uncial

Right: Studies for letter H on a page by White House calligrapher Sanford Fox

Opposite: Exercises completed during the designing of Hallmark Uncial including a decorative border of uncial letters on a printed poster

46

UEHSR
RTSTFL
BNDGJ
AMXKF
PQING
VAWZ

ꝺ ħ
ABCDEFGHIJK

LMNOPQR &
ꟃꞃ q

1 2 3 4 5 6 7 8 9 0 ! ? *

STUVWXYZ
ꟃ

Hallmark Textura—1968/69

Zapf followed a traditional textura model for this alphabet, removing the stodginess apparent in other textura types by his detailing in the junctures and in the elegant waisting of the stems., "enlivened by his calligraphic touch,"[14] as Paul Shaw wrote in his comprehensive treatise "The Calligraphic Tradition in Blackletter Type." Zapf referred to some of his drawings from the '40s and '50s for Hallmark Textura, and there are examples of his studies on printed specimens of newspaper mastheads, as well as a contemporary application of a nineteenth-century blackletter from the Joh. Enschedé typefoundry. Many of the cap forms resemble Cloister Black (issued early in the twentieth century by the American Type Founders Company), which was part of Hallmark's type collection at the time. Hallmark Textura offered a lighter, more refined alternative to Cloister Black and, because it also was used as part of the Stratford and Winchester combinations, more variety.

Albert Kapr in *Fraktur: Form und Geschichte der gebrochenen Schriften*, his 1993 survey of blackletter types, properly described Hallmark Textura as "a modern calligraphic expression of an old form," its ascenders and descenders showing a "pleasure in writing by their endings."[15]

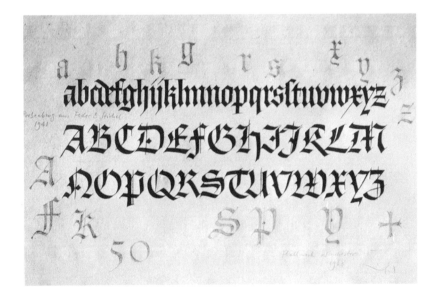

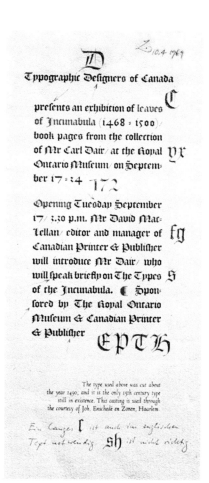

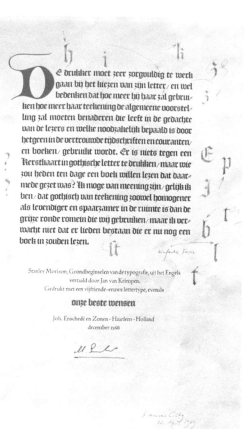

abcdefghijklmnopqrsyuvwxy&z

Opposite: Studies for Hallmark Textura on a page from HZ's *Pen and Graver*

Top: Studies done in Kansas City on a contemporary setting of a 15th century type, and a page designed by Jan Van Krimpen

Left: Pencil drawing for textura caps on a study from 1947

Top: Studies for Hallmark
Textura on an Zapf sketch
for a textura from 1952

Bottom: Early proof of
Hallmark Textura with
comments by HZ

ABCDEFGHI
JKLMNOPQRS
TUVWXYZ

1234567890!?

Everything passes, and what remains of former times, what remains of life, is the spiritual. In everything we do, the claim of the Absolute is unchanging.

PAUL KLEE

* * *

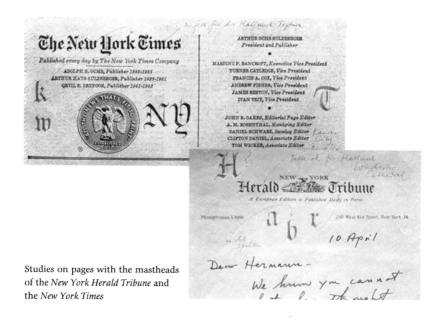

Studies on pages with the mastheads of the *New York Herald Tribune* and the *New York Times*

abcdefghijklmnopqrstuvwxy&z

1234567890!?*

ABCDEFGHIJKLMNOPQRSTUVWY&Z

abcdefghijklmnopqrstuvwxyz!?

ABCDEFGHIJKLMNOPQRSTUVWYZ

1234567890

A B C D
E F G H I
J K L M
N O P Q
R S T U
V W Y Z

SONG

Feare no more the heate o'th' Sur
Nor the furious Winters rages,
Thou thy worldly task hast don,
Home art gon, and tane thy wag
Golden Lads, and Girles all must
As Chimney-Sweepers come to d
Feare no more the frowne o'th' Gr
Thou art past the Tirants stroake,
Care no more to cloath and eate,
To thee the Reede is as the Oake:
The Scepter, Learning, Physicke m
All follow this and come to dust.
Feare no more the Lightning fl.
Nor th' all-dreaded Thunderstone
Feare not Slander, Censure rasl
Thou hast finish'd Joy and mone.
All Lovers young, all Lovers mus
Consigne to thee and come to du
No Exorcisor harme thee,
Nor no witch-craft charme thee.
Ghost unlaid forbeare thee.
Nothing ill come neere thee.
Quiet consumation have,
And renowned be thy grave.

Crown Roman—1969/70

Crown Roman is a clean calligraphic roman with a transitional flavor. It has a companion italic that illustrates more scriptorial qualities than the roman and a handsome set of swash caps that can be used with both the roman and italic lowercase. Reminiscent of Hunt Roman, the proprietary metal type that Zapf designed in 1961 for the Hunt Botanical Library, Crown Roman references the rejected narrow design of his first drawings for the Hunt typeface—the lowercase g, for instance, is very similar in both drawings. It has been suggested that he derived inspiration for the Hunt type from his 1958 calligraphic broadside of Shakespeare's "Cymbeline IV, ii, Guiderius & Arviragus"[16]—and so, by association, the Crown Roman as well. But any direct relationship of either of the designs to the broadside was discounted by Zapf's own statement of it being "one of the so-called developmental pages that precede the making of a type." It was the cumulative effect of many years' experience. Robert Slimbach, the prolific type designer at Adobe Systems, said to me once that it was as if "Hermann distilled all that he had learned from his formal roman calligraphy and lettering into these two designs."[17]

While it is interesting to speculate about the relationship between Hunt Roman and Crown Roman, what can be said for certain is that they each represented, and were designed to accommodate, the technological extremes of type production used at the time—essentially consolidating 500 years into less than a decade—further illustrating Zapf's comfort with changing technology.

Opposite: Calligraphic broadside, one of many studies that influenced the design of Crown Roman

Right: Right: Crown Roman lowercase g (shown in red) compared to the rejected narrow design for Hunt Roman

Right: Copy of HZ's proposal for Missouri, indicating potential ligatures and possible alternate lowercase letters

Below: Page of civiltié from *Pen and Graver* with marginal drawings by HZ

1 2 3 4 5 6 7 8 9 0

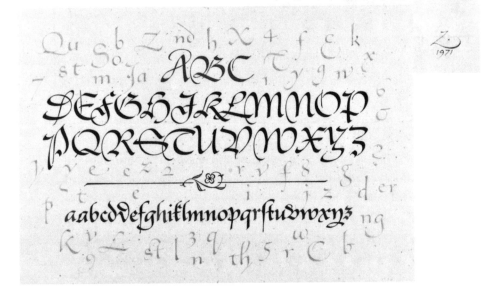

abcdefghijklmnopqrstuvwxyz!?

* 1 2 3 4 5 6 7 8 9 & 0 *

abcdefghijklmnopqrstuvwxyz!?

Missouri — 1970/71

Missouri, one of the more unique types that Zapf designed, is an exotic upright italic with civilité characteristics. Hermann first began to explore this form seriously in 1938 as a model for a contemporary typeface for the D. Stempel typefoundry (never completed) and later with early sketches for his book *Pen and Graver*. Missouri was developed when Zapf began working with Paul Hayden Duensing on the privately-cast Zapf Civilité and can be described as a distant cousin to that typeface. A few of Hermann's sketches for the lowercase of Zapf Civilité show similar letterforms to ones found in the final design for Missouri, although they are lighter overall. Also, Missouri appears narrower but the font sets wide because of the generous exit strokes in many of the lowercase letters. He provided Missouri with two lowercase alphabets.

In a 1985 article from *Fine Print*, Duensing wrote that in Zapf's Civilité, Hermann "embodied the spirit of the historic letterform, while imparting a warm, contemporary feel to the individual letters."[18] In Missouri, Zapf elevates this contemporary feeling. No longer restrained by the conventions of the civilité form, one senses his delight in the making of letters. The caps in particular are striking examples of letter design. Drawn with the assurance of a master scribe, they appear to be influenced more by Hermann's taste and skill than by the inherent logic of the broad-edged pen. He provided two sets of figures — an exuberant old-style, particularly effective when numbers need to command attention, and lining figures that, because their height is smaller than the caps, reconcile nicely when used with the lowercase.

ABCDEFGHIJKLM

It is best to be yourself, imperial, plain & true.

ROBERT BROWNING

NOPQRSTUVWXYZ

Lettering for a dust jacket by HZ with similar characteristics to the final version of Scriptura

Opposite top: Broadside from 1956 by HZ done for Philip Hofer

Opposite bottom: Comparison of Cresci's "cancellarescha testeggiata" with Scriptura

Scriptura—1968/72

Scriptura is an elegant, unconnected script with swash caps, roman caps, and alternate lowercase characters designed to be used at the beginnings of words or lines. Zapf's proposal, rendered with a ballpoint pen, has more of the appearance of handwriting than the final approved design. Its lowercase resembles, in color, the lettering he did for a number of dust jackets for German publishers, as well as the broadside he executed in 1956 using the words of E. A. Lowe (now part of the Philip Hofer Collection at Harvard University's Houghton Library).

Some of the terminals on the ascenders are superficially reminiscent of those advocated by Renaissance writing master Giovan Francesco Cresci for his "cancellarescha testeggiata." The following statement about Cresci and his script by Stanley Morison, from his essay "On Some Italian Scripts of the XV and XVI Centuries," could have been written about Zapf and Scriptura and its effect at Hallmark: "It was [his] manner to elaborate the ascenders …and smooth the angles.… He created a less rigid version of the original [chancery] model which…possessed a degree of sophistication that made it immediately fashionable."[19] When it was introduced, Scriptura's soft, lyrical quality made it a popular choice for typographers at Hallmark, its delicacy providing contrast to the more traditional italic form of Firenze—and additional inspiration for the lettering artists on staff.

ABCDEFGHIJKLM
NOPQRSTUVW
Calligraphy &XYZ
is distinguished by harmony of style·
It is conscious of the methods by which it gets its result·
Its forms are definite·   E·A·LOWE

ABCDEFGHIJK
LMNOPQRST
UVWXY &Z

∗   ∗   ∗

Gran differenza è da l'huoms, che
da gli animali senza ragione', ch
vtili gli animali per lauorare' le
uir la republica, Un semplic
carne' p mangiare', le' forze' p a
lana per vestire', er il late' per
à niuns gioua, nuoce'à tutti, offe.

Gran differenza e da l'huoms,
da gli animali senza ragione,
vtili gli animali per lauorare
uir la republica, Un semplic
carne y mangiare, li forze y
lana per vestine, & il late pe
a niuns gioua, nuoce a turri,

"Cancellarescha testeggiata" (1560)   Scriptura (1972)

Right: Scriptura proposal drawn with a ballpoint pen. HZ's original concept was for the alphabet to have two weights. On this page he identifies possible alternate lower-case letters with red asterisks

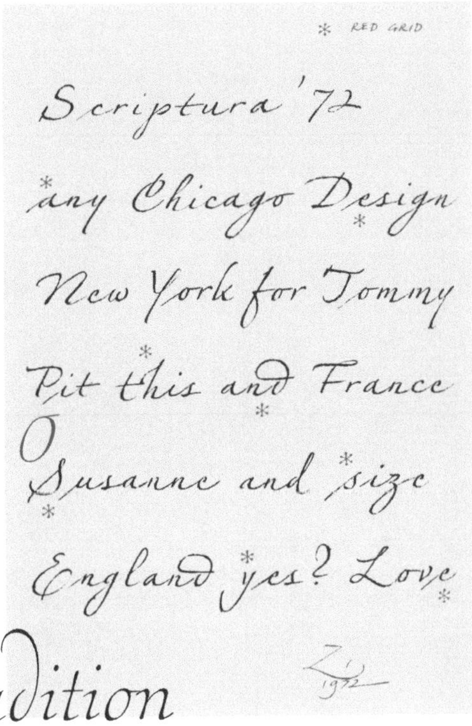

1 2 3 4 5 6 7 8 9 0

Scriptura '72

* any Chicago Design

New York for Tommy

Pit this and France

Susanne and ;size

England yes? Love

A real tradition
is not the relic of the past...
it is the living force that
animates and informs
the future. /

IGOR STRAVINSKY

$A\,B\,C\,D\,E\,F\,G$

$H\,I\,J\,K\,L\,M$

$N\,O\,P\,Q\,R\,S\,T$

$U\,V\,W\,X\,Y\,Z$

a b c d e f g h i j k l m n o p q r s t u v w x y z !?

a b c d e f g h i j k l m n o p q r s t u v w & x y z

Left: Lettering for a dust jacket by HZ with characteristics similar to Scriptura. This and the example shown on page 74 were included in the exhibitions that traveled with *The Art of Hermann Zapf*

ABCDEF
acenmo
GHKLM
NOPRIT
rsuvwx
SUVWZ

Right: Drawing for Shakespeare italic with unit specifications in red

Opposite: Detail of Gudrun's transcription of *The Little Prince* showing similar characteristics to the Shakespeare type

Shakespeare—1967

Added to this distinguished collection was Shakespeare, designed by Gudrun early in Zapf's tenure with the company. It is a simple roman and italic, spiritually related to her Diotima typeface drawn nineteen years earlier and equally revealing of her singular aesthetic. Shorn of any excess, Shakespeare's strength and versatility relies on generous proportions and a sturdy calligraphic line. It appears to be the antecedent of Alcuin, an extended family she designed for digital composition nineteen years later. Both typefaces directly reflect Gudrun's writing with the broad-edged pen. Shakespeare seems especially akin to her 1962 calligraphic piece transcribed from Antoine de Saint-Exupery's *The Little Prince*.[20]

In his introduction to the book *Gudrun Zapf von Hesse*, Dr. Hans Halbey, former director of both the Klingspor and the Gutenberg museums, wrote that even though "the average reader hardly ever notices the qualities of a typeface and often does not even notice the type at all...there is no doubt that each typeface has...its own character and mood, its own spirit, its own style, and its own voice.... Gudrun Zapf von Hesse's work has the right coloration and subliminal quality to be attractive to more than just the expert."[21] It is the last part of Dr. Halbey's analysis that made Shakespeare appealing for Hallmark products and popular with Hallmark's typographers.

A B C D E F G H I J K L M N
a b c d e f g h i j k l m n
O P Q R S T U V W X Y Z
o p q r s t u v w & x y z
1 2 3 4 5 6 7 8 9 0 ! ? *

Bonjour, dit le renard.

Bonjour, repondit poliment le petit prince,

qui se retourna mais ne vit rien.

Je suis la, dit la voix, sous le pommier...

Qui es-tu ? dit le petit prince. Tu es bien joli...

Bonjour, dit le renard.

Je suis un renard, dit le renard.

Bonjour, repondit poliment le petit prin

qui se retourna mais ne vit rien.

Je suis là, dit la voix, sous le pommier…

Qui es-tu? dit le petit prince. Tu es bien.

Simplicity

is the ultimate sophistication.

LEONARDO DA VINCI

A B C D E F G H I J K L M N

a b c d e f g h i j k l m n

O P Q R S T U V W X Y Z

o p q r s t u v w & x y z

*1 2 3 4 5 6 7 8 9 0 ! ? ***

SONNET LX

Stratford Like as the waves make towards the pebbled shore,

Charlemagne So do our minutes hasten to their end;

Winchester Each changing place with that which goes before,

In sequent toil all forwards do contend.

Nativity, once in the main of light,

Crawls to maturity, wherewith being crown'd,

Crooked eclipses 'gainst his glory fight.

And Time that gave doth now his gift confound.

Time doth transfix the flourish set on youth

And delves the parallels in beauty's brow,

Feeds on the rarities of nature's truth,

And nothing stands but for his scythe to mow.

And yet to times in hope my verse shall stand,

Praising thy worth, despite his cruel hand.

William Shakespeare

Stratford, Charlemagne, Winchester—1970

A unique aspect to the Hallmark alphabets designed by the Zapfs—and an illustration of the extraordinary affinity their work has—are what I call the three "phantom" fonts where, by the careful combination of three designs from the original collection, an additional three designs were developed. While similar to what Frederic Goudy did in 1938 when he "created" New Village Text by mixing the lowercase of his Deepdene Text with the capitals of his Tory Text, the Zapf combinations offer more variety than Goudy's combinations. Hermann began with Harald Peter's suggestion that he lighten his original version of Hallmark Textura so its lowercase could be mixed with Gudrun's Shakespeare caps. Zapf called this combination Stratford. Charlemagne, as mentioned earlier, combined the lowercase of Shakespeare with the capital letters from Hermann's Hallmark Uncial. And finally, Winchester was the result of mixing the small capital letters of Hallmark Uncial with the lowercase letters of Hallmark Textura, an approach to blending letterforms that precedes the incunabula and one that Hermann used for numerous broadsides and book titles.

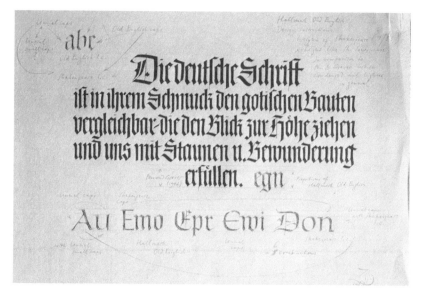

Page from *Pen and Graver* with HZ's sketches indicating type combinations for Hallmark

Constanze — 1968

Besides these original alphabets by the Zapfs, Hermann prevailed upon his friend Joachim Romann, in Kronberg, Germany, to design a script alphabet for Hallmark. It is a variation of the Constanze family of unconnected scripts, including a robust set of initials, that Romann designed for the Klingspor typefoundry in the mid-1950s. Hallmark's Constanze is similar to the medium weight of the earlier metal version but is wider and has a greater degree of slope. Romann included numerous double letter combinations and ligatures and three separate ornamental flourishes with the design. A few years later, McVay designed a condensed version of the alphabet to accommodate Hallmark's narrow greeting card format.

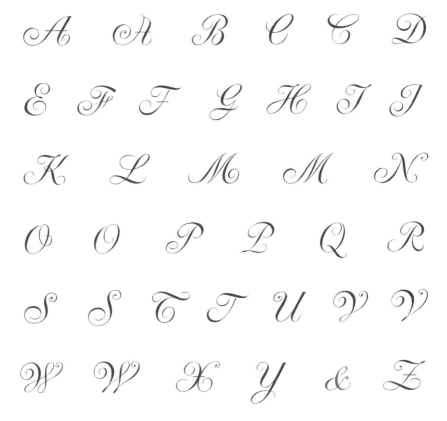

Opposite top: Mailing label for the Klingspor
typefoundry's version of Constanze

Original art for Hallmark's Constanze, drawn by Joachim Romann

S V W

P P M s

1 2 3 4 5
6 7 8 9 0

abcdefghijklmnopqrstuvwxyz

Memoria in aeterna.

ch er ff ij ll pf qu ss th a c d g o r s z ! ?

*   *   *

As a whole, this collection of calligraphically inspired alphabets added a new dimension to the appearance of Hallmark products while providing Hallmark lettering artists with an abundant supply of models to study. It was an education in elegance and the endless possibilities of the broad-edged pen. As I pointed out in the catalog for Zapfest ("Cultivating an Education in Letters"), with these examples Hermann led the staff on a kind of meandering walking tour through the history of written letters—typifying his belief that the past should be transformed into art for our times.

FIVE: HALLMARK EDITIONS

In 1967, the company launched its gift book line, Hallmark Editions. J. C. Hall's interest in books began as a youngster while working in a bookstore in Norfolk, Nebraska, owned by his brothers, William and Rollie. A decade later (as early as 1914), the Hall Brothers retail operation in Kansas City stocked books and other products published by Raphael Tuck & Sons of London. In the early 1960s, Hallmark published a few titles in collaboration with Doubleday and the Swiss fine art publisher Skira. But, according to a 1978 *Publishers Weekly* article by Chandler B. Grannis, Hall's decision to actually publish a line of books was made after he had first considered the acquisition of the Peter Pauper Press.[1] One can understand the appeal for Hall. The philosophy of the Press, founded in 1928 by Peter Beilenson (who, among his other accomplishments, wrote a biography of Frederic Goudy), was "to produce small books, edited to meet variegated interests, distinguished for superior typography, art, and printing, and sold at very low prices."[2] After Beilenson died in 1962, his widow, Edna, who was equally respected in printing and publishing circles, carried on with the business. It was Edna Beilenson who received the offer from Hall, but Grannis records that because of a slight difference of opinion regarding editorial content, "there was no deal."

Coincidently, Rudolf Koch, one of Hermann's early influences, had been fired by the London firm early in his career. (Warren Chappell, a member of Koch's workshop in 1932-33, relayed this anecdote to me in a letter as a hint that, considering Koch's accomplishments after being let go, I might be better off leaving Hallmark.)

Not surprisingly, Harald Peter lobbied J. C. Hall against the acquisition, arguing that the books of the Peter Pauper Press were ersatz versions of those produced by the esteemed German publisher Insel. From the beginning, Insel strove for functional value and aesthetic significance, and used top artists and typographers toward that end—an approach that appealed to both Harald and to Hans Archenhold. Harald recalls that it was Hans who helped convince J. C. Hall that "quality [was] not just printing, but content as well."[3] The original concept of Hallmark Editions was to take advantage of the built-in market and distribution provided by Hallmark stores while enhancing the creative and cultural image of the company.

According to a 1970 article in the *Noon News*, Hallmark's daily publication for its employees, Zapf had been an important contributor to the development of Hallmark Editions. "Several of his best-known typefaces [were] represented in the initial twenty-volume group."[4] Though it is true he was well represented, the phrase "several of his best-known typefaces" is somewhat misleading. I was able to find nineteen of the initial twenty-four titles in the Hallmark archives, only six of which were set in Zapf-designed types; five of these are set in Palatino (both Linotype and Linofilm versions), and the sixth is set in Aldus (Linotype).

Other typefaces used during the early years of the book department (reflecting Harald Peter's classical taste in typography), were Monotype Walbaum (appearing five times), Garamond, Baskerville, Caledonia, and one hand-set in Romanee. Before Hallmark's photocomposition department was well established, Harald, at Zapf's recommendation, used high-quality typesetting firms throughout the United States, such as Franz Hess at Huxley House Ltd., Grant Dahlstrom's Castle Press, and the Plantin Press of Saul and Lillian Marks. Joseph Thuringer of the Rochester Typographic Service also provided typography for a couple of titles, as did Kim Merker, who had recently founded the Windhover Press at the University of Iowa.

Harald looked outside of Hallmark for design help as well but with a bit less success. San Francisco book designer Adrian Wilson, author of *The Design of Books* and *The Making of the Nuremberg Chronicle*, among others, told me in 1974, during one of my visits to his Press at Tuscany Alley, that Harald had approached him early on about designing books for Hallmark. Wilson's award-winning work included commissions from trade publishers and university presses, as well as limited editions, but no agreement with Hallmark was ever reached. A few years later Harald brought in New York designer and letterpress printer Mo Lebowitz to speak to the staff and to discuss the possibility of designing books. Lebowitz's work was less traditional than Wilson's, but his passion for type (and engaging wit) was apparent in everything he did. Still, no agreement was made.

Harald had better luck with artist and designer Norman Laliberté, who in 1968 was teaching at the Kansas City Art Institute. Laliberté was well known for having designed the banners for the

I first met Wilson in 1969 while doing research on the uncial letterform for a project in James Lewis's class at San Joaquin Delta College. Wilson shared Herbert Marcelin's notes regarding a display face they developed for The Oresteia, *published by the Limited Editions Club in 1961.*

Illustration and lettering
for *My Sweet Lord*
by Norman Laliberté

*Laliberté went on to
publish numerous
books, many of them
pertaining to art
education.*

Vatican Pavilion at the New York World's Fair in 1963–64 (and in
doing so, solving the challenge of creating art for a building with
glass walls). His book design, less type-oriented than either Wilson's or Lebowitz's, was distinguished by a vivid sense of color and
experimentation—appropriate for the high-spirited times.

Through hiring and a few transfers from other areas in the
company, Harald assembled a talented and diverse group of book
designers. Illustrations were executed by Hallmark staff artists,

*Holland left soon
after for a successful
freelance career,
eventually influencing
a generation of
illustrators.*

which at the time included Brad Holland, and by respected free-
lancers such as Fritz Kredel, Bernard Fuchs, and Seymour Chwast.
Cartoonists were also called upon, including Charles Barsotti and
Paul Coker, who, like other former Hallmark humor artists, had
found success in syndication and in regular appearances in maga-

zines like *Mad* and the *New Yorker*. Eventually, Hallmark's book offering would expand into a variety of formats, including a successful line of children's books that featured a series of children's classics and close to eighty pop-up and paper mechanical books; one of these was the first book illustrated by celebrated children's book artist Michael Hague just before he left the company.

Hague was at Art Center when I was there, but we didn't meet until he interviewed at Hallmark.

As a consultant, Zapf was occasionally asked to critique the line. Responding to the book department's early efforts after they appeared in the 1967 Drupa Printing Exhibition, he remarked in a letter to Mr. Hall how ideally integrated he thought the design and text were, praising the editorial work led by Webb Schott, then vice president of editorial, and the book design and quality control of Harald Peter, "Always I admire his ideas and the careful execution of the details[5]." In the same letter he also stated how happy he was to be connected with Hallmark's book line—examples of which eventually appeared in an exhibition at New York's Metropolitan Museum of Art, in a show in Paris sponsored by the Louvre, and at most international book fairs. Such recognition pleased J. C. Hall, as revealed in a note he wrote to Harald six years after he retired as president of the company, upon hearing that a Hallmark book had been included in the American Insitute of Graphic Art's (AIGA) best-designed books of 1973, "This is a fine honor and one that is very meaningful to Hallmark and our book line."[6]

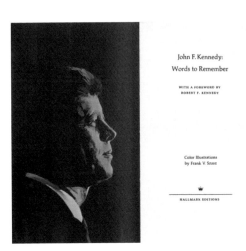

John F. Kennedy:
Words to Remember

WITH A FOREWORD BY
ROBERT F. KENNEDY

Color Illustrations
by Frank V. Szasz

HALLMARK EDITIONS

John F. Kennedy: Words to Remember
Illustration: Frank V. Szasz
Book design: Harald Peter

Spread from *Words To Live By*
Illustration: Fritz Kredel
Book design: Harald Peter

Title spread for *The Rubayyat
of Omar Khayyam*
Illustration: Joseph Isom
Book design: Harald Peter

Spread from *The World of
the Kennedy Women*
Illustration: Bernard Fuchs
Lettering: Norval Arbogast
Book design: Rainer Koenig

Book Design and Calligraphy

Any study of Hermann Zapf's work reveals that few designers have used his and Gudrun's types with more distinction than he has. There are just two examples that he did for Hallmark, both of them small format books in the Hallmark Editions series. The first one he designed was *Thy Sweet Love Remembered*, illustrated by staff artist Bill Greer, who provided nine decorative line drawings for the interior of the book, one for the endliners, and a full-color illustration for the dustjacket. Rich in understatement, the interior is a two-colored jewel imbued with an elegance more commonly found in fine press books. Using a small size of Gudrun's Shakespeare with generous leading, Zapf, in essence, allowed space to heighten the effect of each line. The dust jacket seems slightly incongruous with the book's quiet interior—the intensity of Greer's color overpowers his sensitive line work and appears to have been a concession to what used to be called "pick-up appeal." Neverthe-

Although there is no design credit in the colophon, correspondence and a mockup among Zapf's Hallmark materials at the August Herzog Bibliothek confirms that he did design the book.

From KING HENRY VIII

Song

Orpheus with his lute made trees.
And the mountain tops that freeze.
Bow themselves when he did sing:
To his music plants and flowers
Ever sprung, as sun and showers
There had made a lasting spring.
Every thing that heard him play.
Even the billows of the sea.
Hung their heads, and then lay by.
In sweet music is such art.
Killing care and grief of heart
Fall asleep, or hearing die.

46

Spread from *The Sweet Love Remembered*
Illustration: Bill Greer

Thy Sweet Love Remembered

The Most Beautiful Love Poems

and Sonnets of

William Shakespeare

Selected and Arranged by Dorothy Price
With Drawings by Bill Greer

✦ HALLMARK EDITIONS

SONNET XIV

Not from the stars do I my judgment pluck,
And yet methinks I have astronomy;
But not to tell of good or evil luck,
Of plagues, of dearths, or seasons' quality;
Nor can I fortune to brief minutes tell,
Pointing to each his thunder, rain, and wind,
Or say with princes if it shall go well
By oft predict that I in heaven find;
But from thine eyes my knowledge I derive,
And, constant stars, in them I read such art
As truth and beauty shall together thrive,
If from thy self to store thou wouldst convert;
Or else of thee this I prognosticate:
Thy end is truth's and beauty's doom and date.

8

SONNET XV

When I consider every thing that grows
Holds in perfection but a little moment,
That this huge stage presenteth nought but shows
Whereon the stars in secret influence comment;
When I perceive that men as plants increase,
Cheered and check'd even by the self-same sky,
Vaunt in their youthful sap, at height decrease,
And wear their brave state out of memory;
Then the conceit of this inconstant stay
Set you most rich in youth before my sight,
Where wasteful Time debateth with Decay
To change your day of youth to sullied night;
And all in war with Time for love of you,
As he takes from you, I engraft you new.

9

Top: Title spread from *The Sweet Love Remembered*
Bottom: Typical typographic spread

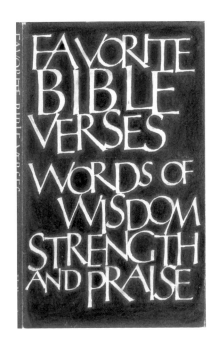

Top left and bottom: Alternative treatments
for *Favorite Bible Verses*

Top right: Alternative sketch for dust jacket
(not used)

less, the book was chosen as one of the AIGA's Fifty Books of 1968, and its appearance in the show's elegant catalog marked an auspicious beginning for Hallmark's young book department. Hermann was especially pleased with the quality of the printing.

The second book, which I was fortunate enough to assist him with, was *Favorite Bible Verses: Words of Wisdom, Strength and Praise,* designed in 1973 and published in 1974. I had just transferred to the book department from the Alphabet Group, and Harald Peter assigned me as a liaison to see the book through final layout and approval once a direction for the illustrations was determined. Hermann had already begun working on it before I joined the project, offering two different treatments for the illustrated verses—a painterly approach, suggestive of stained-glass windows, and a more purely calligraphic direction.

The chosen version, set in Crown Roman, features twelve calligraphic plates integrating an appropriate symbol with each verse.

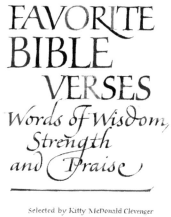

Left: Alternative color proposal for title page

Right: Final hardback cover design

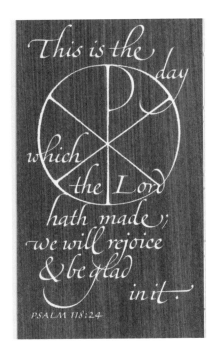

FAVORITE
BIBLE
VERSES
*Words of Wisdom,
Strength
and Praise*

Selected by Kitty McDonald Clevenger

Calligraphy by Hermann Zapf

♛ HALLMARK EDITIONS

PRAISE

THIS IS THE DAY
This is the day which the Lord hath made; we
will rejoice and be glad in it.
   Blessed be he that cometh in the name of the
Lord: we have blessed you out of the house of
the Lord.   *Psalm 118:24, 26*

SING UNTO THE LORD
O come, let us sing unto the Lord: let us make a
joyful noise to the rock of our salvation.
   Let us come before his presence with thanks-
giving, and make a joyful noise unto him with
psalms.
   For the Lord is a great God, and a great King
above all gods.
   In his hand are the deep places of the earth: the
strength of the hills is his also.
   The sea is his, and he made it: and his hands
formed the dry land.
   O come, let us worship and bow down: let us
kneel before the Lord our maker.
   For he is our God; and we are the people of his
pasture, and the sheep of his hand.... *Psalm 95:1-7*

32

Title spread and section opening
for *Favorite Bible Verses*

*Let your light
so shine
before men,
that
they may see
your good works,
and glorify your
Father which is
in heaven.*

ST. MATTHEW 5:16

THE GREATEST OF THESE

Though I speak with the tongues of men and of angels, and have not charity, I am become as sounding brass, or a tinkling cymbal.

And though I have the gift of prophecy, and understand all mysteries, and all knowledge; and though I have all faith, so that I could remove mountains, and have not charity, I am nothing.

And though I bestow all my goods to feed the poor, and though I give my body to be burned, and have not charity, it profiteth me nothing.

Charity suffereth long, and is kind; charity envieth not; charity vaunteth not itself, is not puffed up,

Doth not behave itself unseemly, seeketh not her own, is not easily provoked, thinketh no evil;

Rejoiceth not in iniquity, but rejoiceth in the truth;

Beareth all things, believeth all things, hopeth all things, endureth all things.

And now abideth faith, hope, charity, these three; but the greatest of these is charity.

1 Corinthians 13:1-7, 13

5

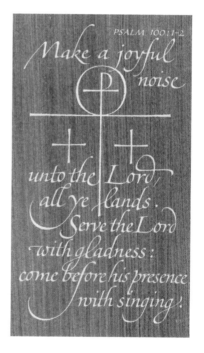

Section opening and two plates
for *Favorite Bible Verses*

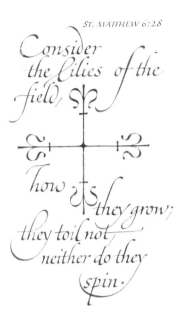

ST. MATTHEW 6:28

Consider the lilies of the field, how they grow; they toil not, neither do they spin.

1 JOHN 4:7

Beloved, let us love one another: for love is of God; and every one that loveth is born of God, and knoweth God.

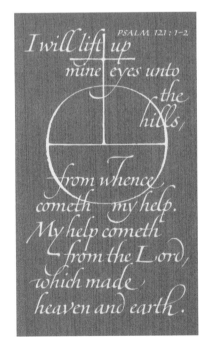

PSALM 121:1-2

I will lift up mine eyes unto the hills, from whence cometh my help. My help cometh from the Lord, which made heaven and earth.

ST. MATTHEW 6:13

For thine is the kingdom, and the power, and the glory, for ever. AMEN.

Illustrations from *Favorite Bible Verses*

78

While the Shakespeare book evokes a sense of serenity in its restraint and subtle use of space, *Favorite Bible Verses* is remarkable in its exuberance and effective use of calligraphy as illustration, though at all times respectful of its message. Zapf celebrates the sacred by exploiting the flexibility of italic letters within a word or a line of text, altering weights and forms where he feels it necessary. It is a lesson about traditional calligraphic forms being allowed to live and breathe, rather than being frozen with thoughtless repetition—another of Zapf's "lessons by example" for the staff. His use of variegated color on half of the plates anticipates a favorite technique of calligraphers practiced to this day.

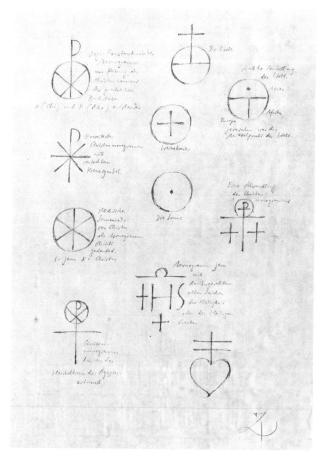

Study for symbols used in *Favorite Bible Verses*

Hermann Zapf   Designer   Bernhard Mannfeld Weg 24   Frankfurt am Main 70   Germany

April 23, 1969

Dear Mr. Hall:

My proposals for the Graphic Arts Museum in the Crown Center, Kansas City, Missouri:

Hallmark Museum of Creative Design (to separate the term clearly from industrial design).
Hallmark Museum of the Creative Arts
The Hallmark Museum of Alphabet.   Perhaps of Alphabet Design but not of Types.   Type
means letterpress printing in general and is perhaps too much in the technical direction
of printing presses, etc.

Basic concept:
The Hallmark Museum of Creative Design should be more connected with the art of letter
design, the tradition of script lettering and handwriting in the United States and abroad.
Writing masters of the past, early lithography, 19th century designs of letters, Spencerian
etc., etc. In general, the new museum should be devoted to the creative aspects and not
on machinery and the technical developments.   The collection should be used for research.
Young people should have opportunities for inspiration and to study the art of lettering in
this country.

A permanent collection could show the historical development of the alphabet, especially
handwriting and creative calligraphy.

Research library
Special collections of books of contemporary alphabet design, lettering and calligraphy.
Children's books (old and new) on an international basis: Czechoslovakia (Jiri Trnka),
Poland, India, Japan, etc.

Display
Additional pages of illuminated manuscripts in color slides. (As the prayerbook of
Catherine of Cleve was displayed some years ago in the Pierpont Morgan Library,
New York). The problem in exhibiting a book is always the same.   Normally one can
show only a double page.

Special collections
Lettering material (available in the files of Hallmark) of outstanding quality. Material
should be collected of internationally known artists of type and alphabet design: Andrew
Szoerke, Frederic W. Goudy (besides the collection of the Rochester Institute of Technology),
William Dwiggins (material must be at the Mergenthaler Linotype Company in Plainview,
New York). Victor Hammer. He died a few years ago and was a great artist and crafts-
man. His widow has a lot of unknown material, which is only shown to close friends of
Victor (Address: Carolyn Hammer, 24 Market Street, Lexington, Kentucky). Jan van
Krimpen, designer. (His Lutetia alphabet was recently sold to the Museum Meermanno-
Westreenianum, The Hague, Netherlands, Prinsessegracht 31 for $10,000).

This report was done from memory only on my way from Kansas City to Pittsburgh,
Pennsylvania. If more details and information are wanted, please write to my Frankfurt
address.

Sincerely yours,

SIX: UNFINISHED PROJECTS

Besides the *Hallmark Lettering Instruction Book*, there were other projects in which Zapf took part, either as a designer or consultant, that for one reason or another were not pursued or completed. A series of typographic ornaments had been considered and dropped, as well as additional alphabet proposals. There was even some consideration of publishing the Bible. According to Harald it had been on the "back burner" for years but was never given priority and, in fact, the only indication of it I could find was a very rough pencil sketch by Hermann for a title page.

One particularly tantalizing idea, at least to me, was a museum dedicated to design—more specifically to lettering design. Since the mid-1970s, when I began putting together a tribute to Ray DaBoll and found myself with examples of his and other artists' work and no place to adequately store them, I have felt that a museum emphasizing the letter arts with recurring exhibits of contemporary and historical works was needed in the United States. I often referred to it as "Klingspor West," in honor of the Offenbach-am-Main institution founded in 1953, whose magnificent collection of lettering, calligraphy, and other book arts has made it a favorite destination of students and professionals from around the world.

Established in 1539, the Pablos press (purported to have been the first in North America) was responsible for the first book known to have been printed in the Western Hemisphere.

Papers in the Hallmark archives indicate that the Hallmark museum might have included the historic Juan Pablos press of Mexico City, which, along with over 40,000 items of printed matter, was on the market at the time the museum was being discussed. Zapf provided Hallmark with a detailed account of the most respected museums and libraries with collections around the world, noting their specialties and recommending ways to differentiate the Hallmark idea. The museum was mainly to be devoted to the aesthetics of letter design rather than technology. In a 1969 letter to J. C. Hall, Zapf briefly outlined the basic concept:

> The Hallmark Museum of Creative Design should be more connected with the art of letter design, the tradition of script lettering and handwriting in the United States and abroad. Writing masters of the past, early lithography, nineteenth century

designs of letters, Spencerian, etc. In general, the new museum should be devoted to the creative aspects and not on machinery and the technical developments. The collection should be used for research. Young people should have opportunities for inspiration and to study the art of lettering in this country.... A permanent collection could show the historical development of the alphabet, especially handwriting and creative calligraphy.[1]

Neither Zapf nor anyone from Hallmark remembers why the idea was dropped, nor could I find anything relevant in the archives. There may have been some question about the authenticity of the press offered for sale. (Even the now-defunct Juan Pablos Museum in Mexico had only a replica on display.) The consensus is that the Hallmark museum was considered too expensive an undertaking. However, it is still an idea worth exploring. As Robert K. Logan pointed out in his book *The Alphabet Effect*, "The alphabet is one of the most valuable possessions in all of Western culture.... It has influenced the development of our thought patterns, our social institutions, and our very sense of ourselves."[2] The popularity of lettering-focused exhibitions over the past few decades, both here and abroad, attests to the fascination of the general public for the alphabet and its formation. With Hallmark's resources behind it and Hermann Zapf's endorsement, a museum celebrating the alphabet's evolution and artistic development had the potential of becoming another popular cultural institution in the Kansas City community.

Not long after I began working at Hallmark, Zapf made his last visit to the company as a consultant. During this visit an opportunity arose that allowed me to watch him work and to have him comment on some of my efforts when we were each given inspirational quotations to interpret for possible card ideas. He chose a piece by Kahlil Gibran, whose writing was particularly popular at the time. He rendered the calligraphy at a small size on rice paper and then had it enlarged to accentuate the textured edges of the letters. The final design was silk-screened in-house and passed out to the staff, but it was never applied to a particular product. Zapf included the print in various publications of his

Examples of the public's fascination with letters range from the Museum of Modern Art's successful exhibitions of lettering by modern artists in the early 1960s to the street level, where it is common for sign painters to find themselves surrounded by spectators during the course of lettering on a window or wall.

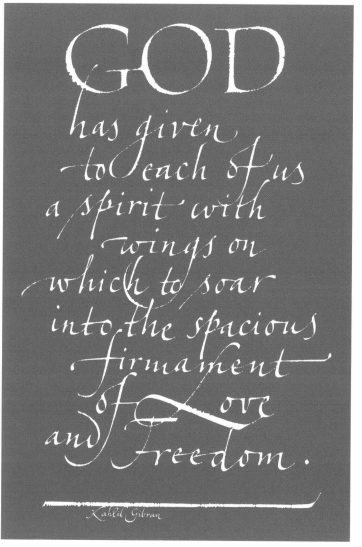

Top: Kahlil Gibran poster designed by HZ during his visit to Hallmark in 1972

Left: Rough idea illustrating international peace by RC for a project with Hermann during same visit

HZ's reconstructed versions of posters sent to Hallmark (ca. 1972); included in the catalog for "The Art of Letters" exhibition at the Grolier Club in 2000

Hermann at the Museo Bodoniano l to r: HZ, unknown, Tibor Szántó, unknown, and Angelo Ciavarella, president of the museum, who is pointing to the Gibran poster seen in the bottom right corner of the photograph.

work and in at least one exhibition he shared with Hungarian book artist Tibor Szántó at the Museo Bodoniano in Parma in 1975. It is visible in a photograph taken during the opening reception that was reproduced in the museum's bulletin that year.

Some months later he submitted a collection of calligraphic poster ideas to Hallmark. These designs, like the ones in *Favorite Bible Verses*, integrated a graphic symbol with quotations but were more varied in contrast and style, reflecting the variety of his text sources. Two of them memorialized the first landing on the moon by Neil Armstrong. Inspirational quotations by Thomas Jefferson, Walt Whitman, Hermann Hesse, Franz Pahnem, Billy Graham, and Martin Luther King, Jr. were also included. Zapf proposed that they be silk-screen-printed on acetate so that they could be displayed in windows. The calligraphy on his proposals, written with tempera directly on acetate, didn't properly adhere to the material, and by the time they arrived from Frankfurt, pieces of lettering had flaked off in varying degrees. Even in that condition one could learn from the work. There was a brief discussion about having me "repair" some of the lettering on prints that Myron McVay made from the originals. Why, I don't recall, unless it was to get some of them to a state in which they could be proofed for further consideration. In the end, the idea was abandoned and the designs were returned. In 2000, Hermann included four versions of the designs in the catalog for his exhibition, "The Art of Letters," held at New York's Grolier Club.

Myron was either too busy or felt I would benefit from the exercise.

85

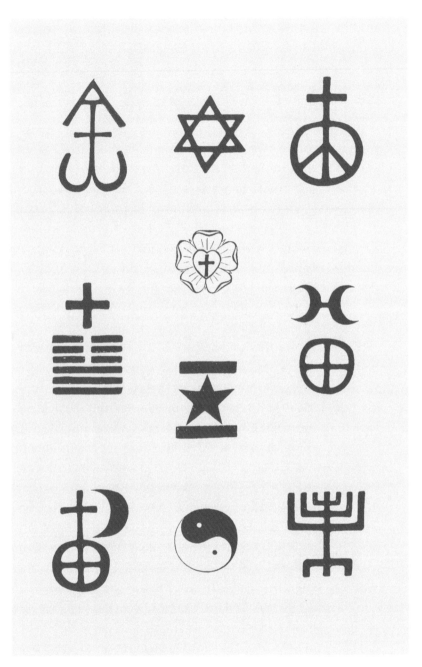

The universality of HZ's proposed series of
posters printed on acetate is reflected in
these images, reduced and cropped from his
original sketches

The Secretaries act in their bureaus for you, not you
here for them. The Congress convenes every Twelfth-
month for you · Laws, courts, forming of States,
the charters of cities, the going and coming of
commerce and mails, are all for you. ❖ List close
my scholars dear · Doctrines, politics & civilization exurge from you · Sculpture and monu-
ments and any thing inscribed anywhere are
tallied in you ·

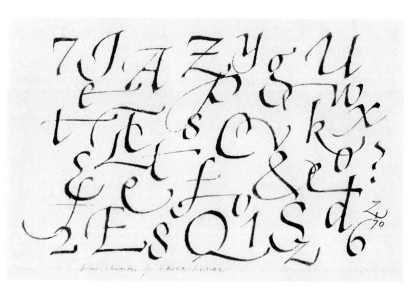

Proposed typographic material not acquired
by Hallmark, including an informal calligraphic
roman alphabet, a series of ornaments, and
swash characters for Crown Roman

Zapf had an "ultra-fine point red ballpoint pen...that he would use to design letters ACTUAL SIZE. Like ten point type drawn by hand, one pass, totally awesome!"[1] Thus recalls Jim Parkinson more than thirty-five years after he first watched Hermann work. He was equally impressed on a different occasion. Known almost as much for his pranks at Hallmark as for his artwork, Parkinson remembers one day feeling particularly unappreciated, so he spent part of the day drawing his version of an "organizational chart," with a mass of jumbled boxes filled with job titles for everyone from the "No Talent-Good Looks Designer" to the "Light Bulb Ladder Man." At the bottom, "underneath a gazillion boxes, there was a single tiny box labeled Artist, with dozens of lines connecting to it from above."[2] He then displayed it prominently in his cubicle so that anyone who stopped by couldn't miss it. Zapf, appreciating the humor and, no doubt, the contrast that his idyllic one-man studio offered, asked ("in front of all the big shots")[3] for a signed copy of the drawing to hang in his studio. For Parkinson, it spoke volumes about the "inner Hermann." It also illustrates Sumner Stone's recollection of Zapf as being sympathetic to the lettering staff.

Zapf's studio was then situated in a fifteenth century watchtower in Dreieichenhain, not far from his Frankfurt home.

In fact, Hermann's rapport with those he met and worked with at Hallmark was always cordial, and by anyone's measure, the Hallmark/Zapf association was as enjoyable (his equestrian adventure notwithstanding) as it was mutually beneficial. "My time with Hallmark," he once wrote, "was much more than a business relationship in my life."[4] Harald Peter fondly recalls meeting Hermann early in the relationship at the Frankfurt Book Fair and the two of them enjoying dinner with "the famous Bohemian Man of the Alphabet, Oldrich Hlavsa."[5] Author of *A Book of Type Design*, Hlavsa had been given the rare permission to come across the Iron Curtain to receive a special prize in Frankfurt. Noel Gordon, who attended a couple of conferences in Sweden as Zapf's guest, discovered that such conviviality was not uncommon. "Needless to say, Hermann is so well known all over the world, we were 'wined and dined' in grand style."[6] He remembers Hermann

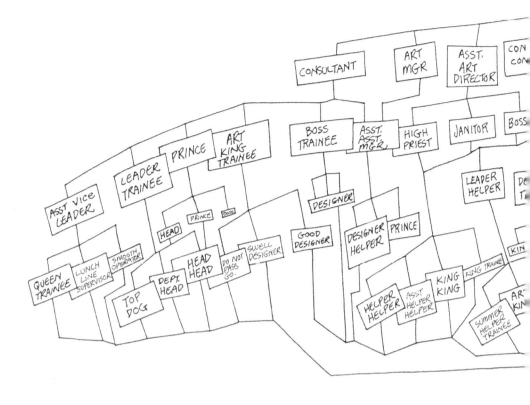

The chart contains the following labels: CONSULTANT, ART MGR, ASST. ART DIRECTOR, CON CON, BOSS TRAINEE, ASST. ASST. MGR, HIGH PRIEST, JANITOR, BOSS, PRINCE, ART KING TRAINEE, LEADER TRAINEE, DESIGNER, LEADER HELPER, DE T, ASST VICE LEADER, PRINCE, BOSS, GOOD DESIGNER, DESIGNER HELPER, PRINCE, KIN, QUEEN TRAINEE, LUNCH LINE SUPERVISOR, SMOOTH OPERATOR, HEAD, DEPT HEAD, HEAD HEAD, DO NOT PASS GO, SWELL DESIGNER, KING KING, KING TRAINEE, TOP DOG, HELPER HELPER, ASST HELPER HELPER, KING KING, AR KIN, SUMMER HELPER TRAINEE

introducing him to a number of respected designers and educators during these trips, like Bror Zachrisson, director of the Grafiska Institutet in Stockholm, and Erik Lindegren, who had recently expanded his book *Vara Bokstaver* into the three-volume *ABC of Lettering and Printing Types*, one of the more elegant anthologies regarding the lettering arts. On another trip, while Hermann and Gudrun attended a family function, Noel spent a day alone in Zapf's studio "atop the watchtower,…with his tools of the trade, his library, and his well-stocked wine cellar."[7]

He remembers, too, "great discussions and lots of fun up in the penthouse" during Hermann's annual visits to Hallmark. On one such occasion, Hermann had a new diamond stylus and wanted to try it out on some glass, "so we went to the cupboard, pulled out some Steuben glass goblets…and Hermann proceeded to engrave his initials into the bottoms."[8]

The monogrammed goblets have gone missing from the penthouse, but I do remember seeing them one evening just a few

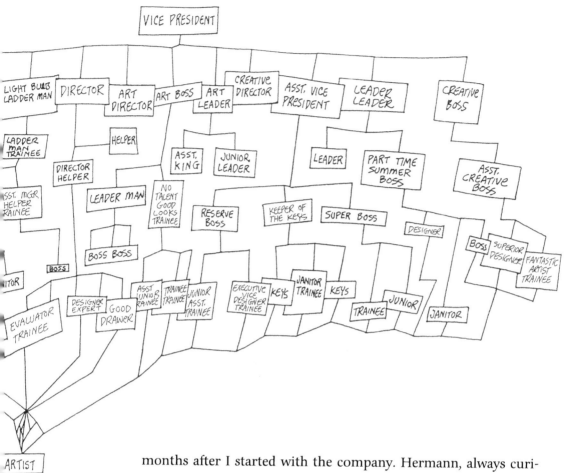

The boxes in the organizational chart read: VICE PRESIDENT, LIGHT BULB LADDER MAN, DIRECTOR, ART DIRECTOR, ART BOSS, ART LEADER, CREATIVE DIRECTOR, ASST. VICE PRESIDENT, LEADER LEADER, CREATIVE BOSS, LADDER MAN TRAINEE, HELPER, DIRECTOR HELPER, ASST. KING, JUNIOR LEADER, LEADER, PART TIME SUMMER BOSS, ASST. CREATIVE BOSS, ASST. MGR HELPER TRAINEE, LEADER MAN, NO TALENT GOOD LOOKS TRAINEE, RESERVE BOSS, KEEPER OF THE KEYS, SUPER BOSS, DESIGNER, BOSS, SUPERIOR DESIGNER, FANTASTIC ARTIST TRAINEE, ITOR, BOSS, BOSS BOSS, ASST. JUNIOR TRAINEE, TRAINEE TRAINEE, JUNIOR ASST. TRAINEE, EXECUTIVE VICE DESIGNER TRAINEE, KEYS, JANITOR TRAINEE, KEYS, JUNIOR, JANITOR, EVALUATOR TRAINEE, DESIGNER EXPERT, GOOD DRAWER, TRAINEE, ARTIST

months after I started with the company. Hermann, always curious about the locales he visited (and invariably possessing some knowledge about them) suggested to McVay that they eat dinner at Kelly's, a favorite pub in Kansas City's historic Westport area. Kelly's is located in a building that originally served as an outfitter in the 1800s, when Westport was one of the main jumping-off points for settlers heading West. McVay and his wife, Tracy, a popular illustrator on staff, invited me to join them and Pat Kahn, a fellow Californian whose calligraphy was as lively as her

Love is something eternal...
the aspect may change, but not the essence.

intellect. But Pat, not yet 21, wasn't allowed into Kelly's, so we stopped at a delicatessen, took our food and wine back to the penthouse, and enjoyed the next few hours discussing events of the day, deciphering some of the famous signatures in the pent-

Pat was a student of Lloyd Reynolds at Reed College, although her work showed little trace of it. She enjoyed exploring with tools and materials and eventually moved to London to study at the Central School with Nicolette Gray.

house guestbook, and admiring Alexander Girard's details of interior design—including the garden pond stocked with koi and the white vinyl hardware he designed for the teak and pivot doors.

One of Hermann's most poignant memories during that same visit to Kansas City was a conversation he had in his room in the penthouse with pioneer industrial designer Henry Dreyfuss, who had been on Hallmark's consulting staff since the early 1960s, contributing, according to J. C. Hall, "taste, beauty, and quality to all our endeavors."[9] Hermann recalls the two of them exchanging their views about the future of creative design, "when computerized composition and graphic art was on the horizon."[10] This was just months before Dreyfuss's tragic suicide in 1972.

A Legacy Established

As pleasant as the penthouse discussions and events were, they tended to be small gatherings. Most artists' exposure to Hermann was through his annual presentations regarding everything from a historical comparison of architecture and letterforms to demonstrations on the finer points of letter design. Feeling a record of the latter would be beneficial, Hallmark filmed a series of short (only a few minutes in duration), 8-millimeter black-and-white films showing close-ups of Zapf working with a variety of tools, e.g., chalk on a blackboard, a mechanical flat-leaded pencil, a broad-edged pen, and a ballpoint pen. These were rough cuts shot without sound during his visit in early 1971. An accompanying notebook was put together by lettering artist, Dale Wittenborn (another former student of Father Catich's), describing each film's contents, noting relevant points of interest, and referencing the *Hallmark Lettering Instruction Book* for further study. But since this book was never published, the films were never incorporated into any kind of formal training program.

The presentation Hermann gave on his last official visit in 1972 included examples of one of the methods he used when ex-

Dale, the first of Catich's students on staff, went on to found the successful Kansas City ad agency, Kuhn & Wittenborn, with Whitey Kuhn, another lettering department alumnus.

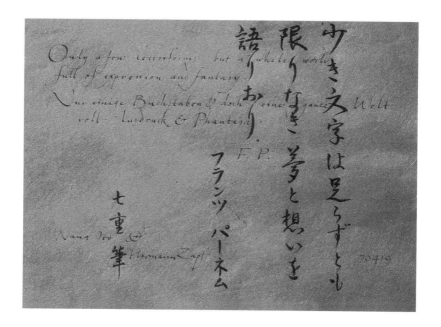

少き文字は足らずとも

限りなき夢と想いを

語りおり

フランツ・パーネム

七重の筆

F.P.

Only a few letterforms but a whole world full of expression and fantasy.

Nur einige Buchstaben & doch eine ganze Welt voll Ausdruck & Phantasie.

Nanae Ito Hermann Zapf

ploring ideas for new typefaces—drawing his thoughts in the margins of printed type specimens, his or someone else's. Calligraphic exercises written on reproductions of historical manuscripts also were shown during this talk, as well as work of a more extemporaneous nature—pieces that began as momentary inspirations at a particular location he might be visiting, using the materials at hand, then completed later in his studio.

Opposite: Playful initials by Pat Kahn. Few lettering artists on staff approached her inventiveness

Top: Calligraphic exercise by HZ and Hallmark artist Nanae Ito, whose calligraphy can also be seen in the *The Art of Hermann Zapf*

Bottom: A few sketches of several for a bookplate designed by HZ for Harald Peter. The final design (far right) was made into an embossing stamp

Not long after this visit, a couple of us were asked for the names of calligraphers who might be invited to Hallmark to speak to the lettering staff. By then, Hermann's influence was considerable; calligraphy and fonts inspired by calligraphy and handwriting were routinely considered in design solutions. It was felt that a series of lectures combined with exhibitions of the speaker's works would provide additional inspiration to the staff and be a way to build upon the foundation that Hermann had provided.

Deciding that the classical roman majuscule would be a good starting point, we invited Father Edward Catich to present first—a logical choice because a few former students of his were on staff at the time. Catich provided a synopsis of his book *The Origin of the Serif,* covering the brush's influence on inscriptional lettering, the significance of evenly-cut striations, and his belief in the superiority of shallow versus deep v-cuts. Then he removed his priest's collar and began cutting letters in slate, encouraging us afterward to try our hand at it. His insistence that cutting the letters was easier than writing them convinced none of us who attempted it, but his lecture was persuasive, and the display of his publications and inscriptional stones impressed everyone who saw them.

Arnold Bank was to follow Catich in the series. Like Catich, he was one of the calligraphers I wrote to when I started out. An

For Catich, even striations and shallow v-cuts were the marks of a master. The argument that deep v-cuts aided legibility was invalid in his opinion because letters cut in antiquity were generally painted after they were incised.

Opposite: Fr. Catich's work on display during his visit to Hallmark in 1973

Left: One of Arnold Bank's "Alphabetic Calligraphics," exhibited at Hallmark's headquarters in 1974

Overleaf and page 117: Two slides shown by HZ in his last presentation at Hallmark. The large letters on page 116 were done using his finger-nail on an inked piece of corrugated cardboard

Bank was a Senior Fulbright Fellow at the Royal College of Art in London from 1954 to 1957. He designed the inscription at Rockefeller Center and taught at Carnegie-Mellon University from 1960 to 1984.

erudite speaker on the history and development of writing and respected for his skillful demonstrations, Bank was a Fulbright scholar with broad practical experience, ranging from architectural inscriptions to paintings with historical references to letterforms. He had also been an art director in *Time* magazine's advertising department. It would have been valuable for the staff to hear and watch him, but just before he was scheduled to speak, another corporate reorganization prompted the cancellation of his lecture. Instead, he sent many of his paintings for an exhibition, including some of the seminal "Alphabetic Calligraphics." Bank's uninhibited, exploratory approach, in which he was a pioneer, nicely complemented the precision of Father Catich's work.

Auspicious Times

Hermann Zapf's contractual relationship with Hallmark ran from 1966 to 1973. The conditions that had fostered the association coincided, particularly in the early years, with what had been

95

Lee joined Hallmark in 1939 as assistant to the creative director. When she retired in 1983, she was vice president of corporate design and a member of Hallmark's board of directors, the first woman to be so named.

an extended period of prosperity and unprecedented growth for the company beginning soon after World War II. Employees like Jeannette Lee, who worked through the shortages brought on by the War, were especially appreciative of the economic changes. In an in-house interview from 1991, she recalled this period of corporate history with particular delight. "Business was so good at that time.... It was growing, so it seemed like almost anything we did was successful. We had unlimited funds to do whatever we needed to do. Everybody was open to ideas, we were expanding so, and it was just a wonderful time for creative development."[11]

Indeed, there were numerous product innovations, new business ventures, and corporately sponsored activities initiated during this extended period of time. Though most are beyond the scope of this book, a few bear mentioning to illustrate the environment Jeannette Lee describes and in which Hermann found himself when he first arrived. The best known, perhaps, is the highly acclaimed Hallmark Hall of Fame, television's longest-running and most honored dramatic series. Two more initiatives that continue to be important to the corporation were the establishment of a nationwide network of retail stores (reinforcing J. C. Hall's belief that "a manufacturer must have a retailer's outlook")[12] and, in Kansas City, the groundbreaking of the 85-acre Crown Center complex of retail shops, residences, theaters, and hotels.

There was also the sponsorship of five International Hallmark Art Awards, which began in the early part of this creative period and ran over the course of eleven years, the stated goals of which were to "encourage fine art,…to bring contemporary recognition to artists of today,…and to broaden public appreciation of fine art."[13] A jury of distinguished critics and curators was selected for each competition. By the time the final program was concluded, more than 350 artists from 27 countries had been represented in 100 exhibitions held in nearly 40 museums throughout the nation. A number of the paintings were purchased by Hallmark, forming the nucleus of the Hallmark Fine Art Collection, which today also includes sculptures and prints, as well as a renowned photography collection—much of which employees see daily as they walk through the hallways and lobbies at headquarters.

Certainly, the corporate-sponsored film and traveling exhibitions of Zapf's work, and the consideration of a museum dedicated to the alphabet and the art of lettering, were further examples of the general optimism described by Jeannette Lee.

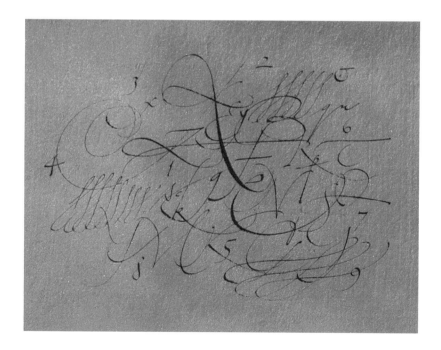

Converging Beliefs

In 1966, the year *The Art of Hermann Zapf* was made, J. C. Hall retired as president of the company that he started with a shoebox full of postcards fifty-six years earlier. (He remained chairman of the board until his death in 1982 at age 89.) Hermann Zapf was the last creative consultant hired while J. C. Hall was actively running the company. Both Zapf and Hall believed in the beneficent promise of their life's work. For J. C. Hall, the significance of a greeting card was that it could "create, enhance, and often rebuild friendships and associations," its shared sentiment representing "open lines of communication that might otherwise be closed."[14] Hermann Zapf's concerns have always gone beyond the design of letters and their arrangement on the page. He ends his autobiography with: "If the letters daily produced by the millions in the printing presses were to be used for only one good purpose every day, then...all the pains we have taken with their creation will have been rewarded."[15] It is easy to see how this confluence of ideals could lead to a successful relationship.

Chappell's books, Anatomy of Lettering, A Short History of the Printed Word, *and* The Living Alphabet, *range in topics from the evolution of printing to the soul of the alphabet. He designed the popular Lydian types in 1938 and Trajanus in 1945 (for which HZ designed a companion Cyrillic in 1957).*

Eminent book artist Warren Chappell, whose published observations of the graphic arts were both broad and deep, once wrote to me that he admired the writing of Renaissance master

98

Opposite: Alphabets drawn with a ballpoint pen for *The Art of Hermann Zapf,* given to Noel Gordon when the film was finished

Left: Calligraphic exercise by HZ shown during his last presentation to the Hallmark lettering staff in 1972

Raphael—a papal scribe before Julius II made him a painter to the palace—because Raphael "never let the pen get bigger than he was."[16] It seems an apt description of Hermann Zapf. Despite the legendary command of hand, refined sense of space, and distinctive stream of elegant letterforms, Hermann never allows his virtuosity to overpower the message before him. He believes that lettering is first of all a communication tool, "not merely artistic expression with letterforms or an instrument of aesthetic values."[17] It is a philosophy that raised expectations for lettering, typography, and type design at Hallmark and goes to the heart of the memo J. C. Hall wrote more than forty-five years ago.

A real tradition is not the relic of a past that is irretrievably gone; it is a living force that animates and informs the present.

– IGOR STRAVINSKY

Acknowledgments

I am grateful to Hermann and Gudrun Zapf for lending me material for this book and for their friendship and generosity over many decades. Thanks to Sumner Stone for sharing his impressions and agreeing to contribute the Foreword, and to Jim Parkinson for his good-humored recollections and for allowing me to use his "organization chart." Noel Gordon and Harald Peter provided important information regarding the beginning of the Zapf/Hallmark association and generously shared correspondence, artwork, and photographs. My gratitude also goes to John Prestianni for editing an early draft of the manuscript and for his valuable insights and criticism.

Sharman Roberts, and the Hallmark Archives staff, Chris Darst, Michelle Spaw, Lynley Farris, and Jeff Smith, were extremely helpful with primary source material. Marina Arnold of the Herzog August Bibliothek in Wolfenbüttel, Germany, and Katharina Maehler, curator of its Hermann Zapf Collection, kindly made available pertinent Hallmark material and provided digital files. Tod Swormstedt, formerly of *Signs of the Times* magazine, confirmed information in Paul Vandervoort's series on calligraphy, and Jorge de Buen provided facts regarding the Juan Pablos Press. Kelli Bruce Hansen, librarian at the University of Missouri Special Collections Department, helped find the *Publishers Weekly* article about J. C. Hall and the Peter Pauper Press.

For providing files and/or permissions to reproduce art, I am thankful to David Pankow, Jerry Kelly, Otmar Hoefer, Pat Kahn, and Philip A. Metzger. Jill Bell assisted in many ways, including tracking down the article on calligraphy in the *Wall Street Journal*. A special thanks goes to Toby Kuhn for sharing his expertise in the preparation of this book, Terry Lee for his help preparing the Zapf fonts, and to Molly Q. Cort, managing editor at the the RIT Cary Graphic Arts Press, for her patience and understanding throughout the process. Also, thanks goes to Teriann Drake, senior vice president, creative, at Hallmark, for looking over the book in its late stages and for her generous support.

And finally, in a variety of ways over a period of years, many friends and colleagues assisted with this effort. I gratefully acknowledge them here: Myron McVay, Bill LaFever, Marshall Wagoner, Dale Wittenborn, Whitey Kuhn (thanks, also, for the use of the premises), Nanae Ito, Edda and Rainer Koenig, Susie Taylor, Bud Braman, Barbara and Lee Stork, Alice Koeth, Ed Benguiat, Melissa Rountree, Robert Slimbach, Shelley Shrock, Amber Goodvin, Steve Carter, Dan Foster, Richard Clement, Pat Mitchell, Bruce Higgins, Patricia Cost, Jim Langford, Joe Houston, Paul Gehl, and Joyce Jennings.

Y que no soló   tiene las cuatro
ese [O sea sabio, solo, solicito   y secreto] que dicen que han
de tener los buenos enamorados, sino   todo un abecé entero : si no, escú-
chame, y verás como te le digo de coro. El es, según, yo ove y a mí me, parece,
agradecido, bueno, caballero, dadivoso, enamorado, firme, gallardo, honrado, ilustre,
leal, mozo, noble, onesto, principal, quantioso, rico y las eses que dicen, y luego,
tacito, verdadero, la X no le cuadro, porque es letra áspera ; la Y ya está dicha ;
la Z, zelador de tu honra. — Miguel de Cervantes saavedra : Don Quijote de la Mancha,
Primera Parte, Capítulo XXXIV — If you have fallen into the amorous net, if it is one
of worth and valor who has caught you in it, one who not only has the four s's
[As we should say, sightly, sprightly, sincere and secret] that they say all true
lovers ought to have, but a whole alphabet ... I will repeat it for you ... it goes
like this : Amiable, Bountiful, Courteous, Devoted, Enamored, Faithful, Gallant,
Honorable, Illustrious, Loyal, Manly, Noble, Open, Princely, Qualified, Rich,
and the s's that I have mentioned. And then Trusty, Vera-
cious — the X does not suit him being too harsh a
letter. The Y has already been given,
and Z is for Zealous
of   your
honor
✿

Miguel de Cervantes Saavedra

Top: Original layout and final printed example
of a page from *Orbis Typographicus*

Left: Phil and Hermann looking over a proof
(ca. 1970)

Appendix: Hermann Zapf & The Crabgrass Press

Pressmark designed
by Harald Peter
and cut in wood by
Fritz Kredel

One of the pleasant benefits of Hermann's trips to Hallmark was the opportunity to visit his friend Phil Metzger (1918–1981) at the Crabgrass Press in Prairie Village, Kansas, a suburb of Kansas City. Their friendship began after Phil and his wife Louise visited the Klingspor Museum prior to Hermann's first meeting at Hallmark. They saw each other regularly during Hermann's visits to Kansas City and would often make weekend trips to other private presses in the region, such as Jim Yarnell's Oak Park Press and Bill Jackson's 4 Ducks Press in Wichita, and Carol Coleman's Prairie Press in Iowa City. Phil and Louise, both Chicagoans and children of German immigrants, traveled to Europe often and would visit Hermann and Gudrun during their trips to Germany.

A vice president at the Kansas City Power & Light Company at the time of their meeting, Phil had been a lover of books and fine printing all his life and decided to teach himself to print at the age of 40. (In fact, it became a family affair, with Louise and their sons Philip and Joel learning to print as well.) Over the years, Phil amassed an enviable collection of types from some of the finest European foundries, including Stempel, Enschedé, and Deberny & Peignot. Regarding the name of his press, he once wrote: "The homeowner knows that if he neglects his lawn, it will soon be overrun with crabgrass. Since acquiring my press, I have spent little time on the lawn. Ergo: the Crabgrass Press."

The Metzgers loved to entertain and were known for their parties. During the Christmas holidays they would often have two—one for business associates and one for their "creative" friends, which included many Hallmark artists and educator Rob Roy Kelly, director of the design department at the Kansas City Art Institute and author of *American Wood Types*. Visiting luminaries from the typographical and printing arts, such as R. Hunter Middleton and Paul Hayden Duensing, also visited the shop when they were in town (invariably enjoying one of Louise's delightful meals). One colleague wrote: "Fortunate indeed was the friend who would visit the Metzger household, which became a magnet to draw talent and interesting people from all disciplines of the graphic and book arts from far and near."[1]

Phil also helped Sumner Stone and Dale Wittenborn acquire a press that they used until Sumner left Hallmark.

Phil befriended a number of young designers and was generous with his time to anyone interested in books (he had an extensive library) and fine printing. Harald Peter was a frequent guest, using the press for personal projects and sometimes working there with Hermann. And it was my pleasure to know and collaborate with Phil on projects of mutual interest over the last decade of his life.

Right: Typographic exercise by HZ and Harald Peter set at the Crabgrass Press

Below: Gathering around Phil's Albion press during a party, April 17, 1970. l to r: Harald Peter, Phil Metzger, HZ, Rob Roy Kelly, Bill Jackson and Jim Yarnell

Bottom: Title spread from *Evening Conversations* (1980) featuring a linocut by Bill Jackson and lettering by Rick Cusick

Opposite: Page from *Orbis Typographicus*

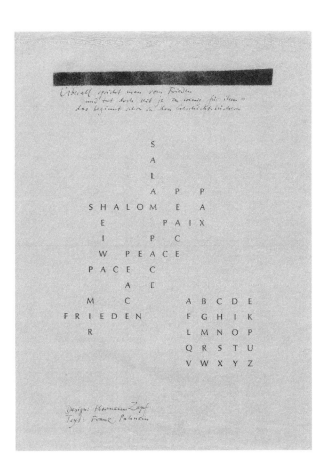

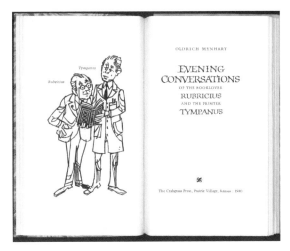

It was during most of those ten years that Phil and Hermann produced the portfolio *Orbis Typographicus: Thoughts, Words and Phrases on the Arts and Sciences*—experimental typography printed on a variety of hand- and machine-made papers. I had the rare opportunity of seeing Hermann's layouts as they arrived—both the early ones, tightly indicated, leaving little to chance, and the later, more casual ones that required more interpretation—and because Phil's eyesight was poor (a result of diabetes brought on by a heart attack), he asked me to look over his proofs before he sent them back to Germany. Hermann's original layouts now reside in the Cary Graphic Arts Library at RIT, a gift from the Metzger family.

Copies of the Orbis *layouts and a complete collection of material printed at the Crabgrass Press are also in the Department of Special Collections, Kenneth Spencer Research Library at the University of Kansas.*

In 1980, the same year the *Orbis* was printed, Phil published a version of Oldrich Menhart's *Evening Conversations*, a dialogue between a printer and a bookseller about the relative attributes of books. First published in Czechoslovakia in 1937, there was a German translation by Otto Babler produced in 1947, and in 1959, Zapf designed an edition published by the Stempel typefoundry, in which each evening's dialogue was set in a different typeface. Hermann secured permissions from all the appropriate parties, including Menhart's widow, so that Phil could translate it (assisted by his son, Phil) and print it in English.

Hermann and Phil were in the beginning stages of another project, *Poetry through Typography*, when Phil died as a result of a second heart attack in 1981. The project was printed in his memory at the Kelly/Winterton Press twelve years later.

The Book of Tea   by Kakuzo Okakura 1862-1913

茶
の
本

The claims of contemporary art cannot be ignored in any vital scheme of life. _____ The art of today is that which really belongs to us: it is our own reflection. In condemning it we but condemn ourselves. _____ We say that the present age possesses no art:- who is responsible for this? It is indeed a shame that despite all our rhapsodies about the ancients we pay so little attention to our own possibilities. _____ Struggling artists, weary souls lingering in the shadow of cold disdain! In our self-centered century, what inspiration do we offer them? _____ The past may well look with pity at the poverty of our civilization; the future will laugh at the barrenness of our art. _____ We are destroying art in destroying the beautiful in life.

Notes

Preface

1. Thomas James Cobden-Sanderson, *Ecce Mundus: Industrial Ideals and the Book Beautiful* (London: Chiswick Press, Hammersmith Publishing Society, 1902).
2. Paul Vandervoort, "Calligraphy: Hermann Zapf," (*Signs of the Times*, August through December, 1979).
3. John Dreyfus and Knut Erichson, *ABC-XYZapf* (London: The Wynkyn de Worde Society, Offenbach: Bund Deutscher Buchkunstler, 1989) pp. 143-146.
4. John Prestianni, *Calligraphic Type Design in the Digital Age* (San Francisco: Ginko Press, 2001) pp. 24-29.
5. Hermann Zapf, in conversation with the author, May 22, 2005.

Chapter One: What Our Lettering Needs

1. Hermann Zapf, in a fax to the author, February 15, 1989.
2. Hans Archenhold, Hallmark oral history, March 31, 1992.
3. Jeannette Lee, in conversation with the author, 1989.
4. J. C. Hall and Curtiss Anderson, *When You Care Enough* (Kansas City: Hallmark Cards, Inc., 1979) p. 256.
5. J. C. Hall, memorandum, June 22, 1964, transcribed verbatim and sent in an email to the author by Noel Gordon, January 15, 2004.
6. J. C. Hall, memorandum, June 22, 1964, transcribed verbatim and sent in an email to the author by Noel Gordon, January 15, 2004.
7. Beatrice Warde, "Printing Should Be Invisible," *The Crystal Goblet* (Cleveland and New York: The World Publishing Company, 1956), pp. 11-17.
8. Noel Gordon, in an email to the author, January 13, 2004.
9. J. C. Hall and Curtiss Anderson, *When You Care Enough* (Kansas City: Hallmark Cards, Inc., 1979) pp. 202-203.
10. Hans Archenhold, Hallmark oral history, June 17, 1992.
11. Hermann Zapf, in conversation with the author, May 22, 2005.
12. Harald Peter, in an email to the author, February 26, 2008.
13. Noel Gordon, in an email to the author, January 13, 2004.

Chapter Two: The Art Of Hermann Zapf & Its Effect

1. "Hermann Zapf and His Work," printed brochure, c. 1966.
2. Noel Gordon, in an email to the author, January 13, 2004.
3. Hermann Zapf, *About Alphabets* (Cambridge: MIT Press, 1970) p. 76.
4. Noel Gordon, in an email to the author, January 13, 2004.
5. Peter Seymour, from an early draft for film in Hallmark archives, March 25, 1966.
6. Sumner Stone in an email to the author, January 2, 2005.
7. "Eminent Designer Views Typography In Terms of Change," *Printing News*, August 2, 1969.
8. Gene Federico, quoted in *Dr Leslie & The Composing Room*, MFA Thesis Project, written & designed by Erin K. Malone, http://www.drleslie.com/.
9. Hermann Zapf, "The Brotherhood of Calligraphers," *With Respect...to RFD*, (Freeport: TBW Books, 1978) pp. 91-92.

10. Fridolf Johnson, "Donald Jackson, calligrapher and illuminator" *American Artist*, Volume 34, No. 5, May 1970.

11. Meg Cox, "If Calligraphers Wrote Headlines, They'd Look Like This" (*Wall Street Journal*), July 14, 1978.

12. Beatrice Warde, The Literary Supplement to *The London Times*, 1965, as quoted by Raymond F. DaBoll in *Recollections of the Lyceum and Chautauqua Circuits* (Freeport: The Bond Wheelwright Company, 1969) p. 94.

Chapter Three: The Lettering Manual

1. Hermann Zapf, *About Alphabets* (Cambridge: MIT Press, 1970) p. 77.

2. Hermann Zapf, Introduction, *The Hallmark Lettering Instruction Book*, Hallmark Archives, 1970, unpublished.

3. Hermann Zapf, *Creative Calligraphy, Instructions and Alphabets, A new instruction manual for learning the art of calligraphy*. Rotring Ltd., 1985.

4. Hermann Zapf, Introduction, *The Hallmark Lettering Instruction Book*, Hallmark Archives, 1969, unpublished.

5. Sumner Stone in an email to the author, January 2, 2005.

Chapter Four: Typographic Transition

1. Jim Parkinson, in an email to the author, June 2, 2002.

2. Hermann Zapf, in conversation with the author, May 22, 2005.

3. Myron McVay, Hallmark oral history, November 1993.

4. Jim Parkinson, in conversation with the author, October, 1999.

5. Harald Peter, in an email to the author, February 26, 2008.

6. Myron McVay, Hallmark oral history, November 5, 1993.

7. Frank Romano, "The Phototypesetting Era," *Printing History: The Journal of the American Printing History Association*. (Volume XXIII, No. 2, 2003) p. 42.

8. Noel Gordon, in a letter to Hermann Zapf, January 13, 1966.

9. Hermann Zapf, in conversation with the author, May 22, 2005.

10. Hermann Zapf, *About Alphabets*, (New York: The Typophiles, 1960) p. 45.

11. Jim Parkinson, in an email to the author, June 2, 2002.

12. Jim Parkinson, in an email to the author, June 2, 2002.

13. Jeannette Lee in conversation with the author, 1989.

14. Paul Shaw, "The Calligraphic Tradition in Blackletter Type," (*Scripsit*, 1999) p. 44.

15. Albert Kapr, *Fraktur: Form und Geschichte der gebrochenen Schriften* (Mainz: Verlag Hermann Schmidt. 1993) p. 140.

16. Paul Standard, referred to by George H. M. Lawrence in *Hunt Roman: The Birth of a Type* (Pittsburgh: The Pittsburgh Bibliophiles, 1965), p. 10.

17. Robert Slimbach, in conversation with the author, July 2004.

18. Paul Hayden Duensing, "A New Civilité," *Fine Print*, July 1995.

19. Stanley Morison, *Letter Forms* (London: Nattali & Maurice, 1968) p. 149.

20. Hans Halbey, Gudrun Zapf von Hesse, (New York: Mark Batty Publisher, 2002) p. 131.

21. Ibid.

Chapter Five: Hallmark Editions

1. Chandler B. Grannis. "Peter Pauper's Fifty Years" (*Publishers Weekly*, November 27, 1978) p. 37.

2. Chandler B. Grannis, "Peter Pauper's Fifty Years" (*Publishers Weekly*, November 27, 1978) p. 34.

3. Harald Peter, in an email to the author, February 26, 2008.

4. "Zapf's lettering designs combine new, old world style." (*Noon News*, April 22, 1970) p. 1.

5. Hermann Zapf, letter to J. C. Hall, December 27, 1967.

6. J. C. Hall, memo to Harald Peter, June 27, 1973.

Chapter Six: Unfinished Projects

1. Hermann Zapf, in a letter to J. C. Hall, April 23, 1969.

2. Robert K. Logan, *The Alphabet Affect*, (New York: William Morrow and Company, Inc., 1986), p. 18.

Chapter Seven: More Than A Business Relationship

1. Jim Parkinson, in an email to the author, June 2, 2002.

2. Jim Parkinson, in an email to the author, June 2, 2002.

3. Jim Parkinson, in an email to the author, June 2, 2002.

4. Hermann Zapf, in a letter to Jeannette Lee, June 20, 1993.

5. Harald Peter, in an email to the author, February 26, 2008.

6. Noel Gordon, in an email to the author, January 13, 2004.

7. Noel Gordon, in an email to the author, January 13, 2004.

8. Noel Gordon, in an email to the author, January 13, 2004.

9. J. C. Hall and Curtiss Anderson, *When You Care Enough* (Kansas City: Hallmark Cards, Inc., 1979) p. 189.

10. Hermann Zapf, in a letter to Jeannette Lee, June 20, 1993.

11. Jeannette Lee, Hallmark oral history, December, 1991.

12. J. C. Hall and Curtiss Anderson, *When You Care Enough* (Kansas City: Hallmark Cards, Inc., 1979) p. 236.

13. Joyce C. Hall, "The Hallmark Art Award" catalog (Hall Brothers, Inc., 1949) p 5.

14. J. C. Hall and Curtiss Anderson, *When You Care Enough* (Kansas City: Hallmark Cards, Inc., 1979) p. 204.

15. Hermann Zapf, *About Alphabets*, (New York: The Typophiles, 1960) p. 75.

16. Warren Chappell, in a letter to the author, February 10, 1983.

17. Hermann Zapf, "Public Lettering and Visual Pollution," *Hermann Zapf & His Design Philosophy* (Chicago: The Society of Typographic Arts, 1987) p. 107.

Appendix: Hermann Zapf & The Crabgrass Press

1. Jim Yarnell, "*Phil Metzger: A Tribute Too Late*," spoken memorial to Phil Metzger, Kansas City, September, 1981. Special printing. Wichita, Kansas: Oak Park Press, 1981.

Sources

Anderson, Curtiss. "At Hallmark, They Turn Greeting Cards into Books —And Sometimes the Other Way Around." *Publishers Weekly* 27 December 1976.

The Art of Hermann Zapf. Film produced by Hallmark Cards, Kansas City, MO 1967. http://palimpsest.stanford.edu/byform/ mailing-lists /bookarts/2004/01/msg00259.html

Artograph: Hermann Zapf. 1.1 New York: Baruch College, 1977.
Bain, Peter, and Paul Shaw, eds. *Blackletter: Type and National Identity*. New York: Princeton Architectural Press, 1998.

Catich, Edward M. *The Origin of the Serif: Brush Writing & Roman Letters*. Davenport, Iowa: Catfish Press, St. Ambrose College, 1968.

Champion Papers: The Printing Salesman's Herald. Book 39 Dedicated to the Work of Hermann Zapf. New York: Champion Papers, 1978.

Chappell, Warren. *The Anatomy of Lettering*. New York: Loring & Mussey, 1935.

—. *The Living Alphabet*. Charlottesville: UP of Virginia, 1975.

—. *A Short History of the Printed Word*. New York: Knopf, 1970.

The Committee for Italic Handwriting Newsletter. New York: Rochester Institute of Technology. Various issues 1960-70.

Cox, Meg. "If Calligraphers Wrote the Headlines, They'd Look Like This: Typewriters Killed the Craft, but Now It Is Back, Hotter than Macramé." *Wall Street Journal* 14 July 1978. Rpt. in *ProQuest Historical Newspapers: The Wall Street Journal* (1889-1989): 1.

Cusick, Rick. *OK? It's All Yours!: Informal Recollections of Arnold Bank*. Kansas City, Missouri: Nyx Editions, 1988.

—. Unpublished correspondence.

—, ed. (uncredited). *With Respect...to RFD: An Appreciation of Raymond Franklin DaBoll and His Contribution to the Letter Arts*. Freeport, Maine: TBW Books, 1978.

Dreyfus, John, and Knut Erichson, eds. *ABC-XYZapf: Fifty Years in Alphabet Design*. London: Wynkyn de Worde Society, n.d.

"Eminent Designer Views Typography in Terms of Change." *Printing News* 2 Aug. 1969: 1+.

The Fine Art of Letters: The Work of Hermann Zapf Exhibited at the Grolier Club New York 2000. Darmstadt: n.p., 2000.

Fine Print on Type: The Best of Fine Print Magazine on Type and Typography. Edited by Charles Bigelow, Paul Hayden Duensing, and Linnea Gentry. San Francisco: Bedford Arts, 1989.

"First Type Directors' Medal to Zapf." *Publishers Weekly* 3 April, 1967: 96.

"Greeting Cards Were Never Like This: Alexander Girard's Apartment
for Hallmark." *Interiors*. n.d.: 100-105.

"Guest Apartment." *Progressive Architecture* February, 1963: 142-47.

Hermann Zapf Narration. Unpublished typescript, n.d.

Kapr, Albert. *Fraktur: Form und Geschichte der gebrochenen Schriften*.
Mainz: Hermann Schmidt, 1993.

Lettering by Modern Artists. New York: Museum of Modern Art, 1964.

Logan, Robert K. *The Alphabet Effect: The Impact of the Phonetic Alphabet
on the Development of Western Civilization*. New York:
William Morrow, 1986.

Morison, Stanley. *Letter Forms Typographic and Scriptorial: Two Essays on
Their Classification, History and Bibliography*. London:
Nattali & Maurice, 1968.

Ogg, Oscar, et al. *Lettering*. Brooklyn: Higgins Ink, 1949.

"A Portrait of the Artist." *Cards Magazine* Spring (1968): 9-11.

Prestianni, John. "Hermann Zapf: A Biographical Portrait." *Alphabet:
The Journal of the Friends of Calligraphy* Winter 1987: 16-23.

—, editor. *Calligraphic Type Design in the Digital Age: An Exhibition in
Honor of the Contributions of Hermann and Gudrun Zapf: Selected Type
Designs and Calligraphy by Sixteen Designers*. San Francisco:
Gingko Press, 2001.

Publishers Weekly Special Design Issue 6 December 1976: 1-43.

Reynolds, Lloyd J. *Straight Impressions*. Compiled by Rick Cusick.
Woodwich, Maine: TBW Books, 1979.

Romano, Frank. "The Phototypesetting Era." *Printing History: The Journal
of the American Printing History Association* 46: 36-47.

Seymour, Pete. *Lettering from A to Zapf*. Unpublished typescript, 1966.

Shaw, Paul. *The Calligraphic Tradition in Blackletter Type*. Special issue of
Scripsit 22.1/2 (1999): 1-48.

Stravinsky, Igor. *Poetics of Music in the Form of Six Lessons*. Trans. by
Arthur Knodel and Ingolf Dahl. Cambridge: Harvard UP, 1942.

Vandervoort, Paul. "Calligraphy." *Signs of the Times Magazine*. N.p.: n.p.,
series, 1967-1981.

Yarnell, Jim. *Phil Metzger: A Tribute Too Late*. Spoken by Jim Yarnell
at Kansas City on September 22, 1981. Special printing. Wichita,
Kansas: Oak Park Press, 1981.

Zapf, Hermann. *About Alphabets: Some Marginal Notes on Type Design*.
New York: Typophiles, 1960.

—. *About Alphabets: Some Marginal Notes on Type Design*. Cambridge:
M.I.T. Press, 1970.

—. *Alphabet Stories: A Chronicle of Technical Developments by Hermann Zapf*
Rochester: RIT Cary Graphic Arts Press, 2007

—. *Creative Calligraphy: Instructions and Alphabets.* Trans. Stephen
Morton and Paul Standard. West-Germany: Rotring-Werke
Riepe, 1985.

—. *Hermann Zapf and His Design Philosophy: Selected Articles and Lectures
on Calligraphy and Contemporary Developments in Type Design,
with Illustrations and Bibliographical Notes, and a Complete List of
His Typefaces,* Carl Zahn, intro. Chicago: Society of Typographic
Arts, 1987.

—. *Pen and Graver: Alphabets and Pages of Calligraphy.* Preface by Paul
Standard; cut in metal by August Rosenberger. New York:
Museum Books, 1952.

— and Philip Metzger. *Obis Typographicus: Thoughts, Words and Phrases
on the Arts and Sciences.* n.p.: Crabgrass Press, 1980.

— and Jack Werner Stauffacher. *Hunt Roman: The Birth of a Type.*
Forward by George H. M. Lawrence. Pittsburgh: Pittsburgh
Bibliophiles, 1965.

Zapf von Hesse, Gudrun. *Bindings, Handwritten Books, Typefaces, Examples
of Lettering, and Drawings.* West New York, New Jersey:
Mark Batty, 2002.

"Zapf's Lettering Designs Combine New, Old World Style." *Noon News*
in-house pub. Hallmark Cards, Kansas City, Missouri, 22 April 1970.

Photography credits:

pg. xii, unknown; pg. 4, unknown; pg. 5, (Andrew Szoeke's wooden block) Jill Bell; pg. 6, Jim Harrison; pg. 9, credited to Charles Eames (reproduced from an article in *Progressive Architecture*, ca. 1962, in the possession of the Hallmark Archives); pg. 10 top, credited to William Reynolds Infinity, Inc. (reproduced from the same article); pg. 10 bottom, unknown; pg. 15, unknown; pg. 85, "Foto TOSI," copyright Museo Bodoniano, reproduced with permission from an article in the museum's 1972 annual report, in the possession of the Hallmark Archives); pg. 94, unknown; pg. 102, unknown; pg. 104, unknown. All photographs of Hermann Zapf used in the chapter opening collages are believed to be by retired Hallmark photographer, Fred Kautt, who was assigned to record the filming of *The Art of Hermann Zapf*, but only the two so-called "frog shots" in the opening design for Chapter Two can be confirmed. Kautt also shot the photograph of the Hallmark headquarters building appearing in the opening for Chapter One. Negatives of the two views of the Dreieichenhain watchtower used in that same design are in the Hallmark Archives and are believed to be stills from the German footage of *The Art of Hermann Zapf* by Heinz Burger.

Index

Editorial and Production by Molly Cort

Book Design by Rick Cusick

Printed by the Rochester Institute of Technology

Printing Applications Laboratory on Mohawk superfine paper

Bound by Hoster Bindery, Inc., Ivyland, Pennsylvania

Composed in Crown Roman and Italic

The pencil sketch below was found in the August Herzog Bibliothek in the

Hermann Zapf files for The Hallmark Lettering Instruction Book.

It's nice to warm up old memories. | HZ